STUDYGUIDE / WORKBOOK

INTRODUCTION TO

FINANCIAL

INFORMATION

SOURCES & INTERPRETATION

Second Edition

Mark J. Minbiole, CPA, MBA, CFP
Vector Publishing
Midland, Michigan 48640

AF887881

Production Editor: Elizabeth A. Minbiole

Cover Design: Eloi B. Nim

Second Edition
First Printing

ISBN: 0-9660030-1-2

Copyright 1999 by Vector Publishing
A division of Vector Enterprises, Inc.
Midland, Michigan 48640-6779

All rights reserved. No part of this book may be reproduced, in any form or by any means, without the express written permission from the publisher. This publication is not intended to provide investment, legal, accounting, financial, tax, investment, or other advice. If any such advice is needed, the advice of a qualified professional should be sought. No legal responsibility for the completeness or accuracy of the contents of this book is assumed.

Printed in the United States of America

Dedicated to Liz and Thomas.

Table of Contents

Preface

Purposes of This Studyguide/Workbook

The two primary purposes of *Introduction to Financial Information: Sources and Interpretation* are:

1. To provide a broad framework for finding and interpreting financial information;
2. To provide a basic studyguide and workbook to accompany *The Wall Street Journal Guide to Understanding Money and Investing.*

The combination of this studyguide/workbook and *The Wall Street Journal Guide to Understanding Money and Investing* is designed to form the foundation for a 2 credit hour course introducing college students to financial information. Other materials will undoubtedly be needed to supplement the information contained in the two aforementioned texts, such as *The Wall Street Journal*, *The Wall Street Journal Educational Edition* ("How To Read Between the Lines"), company Annual Reports, and other business periodicals.

Introduction to Financial Information: Sources and Interpretation introduces the reader to the vast number and variety of financial information sources. Its express purpose is to assist in locating, reading, and interpreting pertinent financial information to develop informed opinions and make decisions. It opens the doors to studying the basic concepts of such wide-ranging disciplines as economics, accounting, law, finance, banking, and investments.

As an introductory text, full-scale analysis of financial data is not the objective. Rather, the objective is to identify various sources of financial information and interpret the information. Basic interpretation is the first step in the full-scale analysis of information.

The steps in the information analysis process can be summarized as follows:

- Identify potential information sources
- Obtain and interpret the information
    - read the information
    - gain basic understanding of the information
    - draw conclusions as to the information's implications

- Analyze the information
    - challenge its biases
    - evaluate its reliability
    - dispute or accept the conclusions

Because the field of financial information expands continuously at an extremely rapid pace, this studyguide/workbook can only begin to introduce the reader to the most significant current sources of financial information. But with this introduction, exploration of other financial information not addressed here should prove to be easier.

"What financial information would I like to have before making this decision?" This query forms the foundation of this book. When the reader is faced with a decision that involves financial information, s/he should ask this key question. This book investigates these various sources of information, as well as serving as a basic introduction to the interpretation of the financial information we have sought and found.

Chapter Format

Each chapter is designed using a basic format:

- chapter concepts
- background
- topic material
- supplemental readings
- outline for corresponding section in: *The Wall Street Journal Guide to Understanding Money and Investing*
- chapter summary
- key terms
- review questions
- exercises
- problems/cases
- materials for further reference
- Internet web sites and search engines to explore

Not every chapter will have each of the aforementioned sub-parts.

Purposes of Appendices

Each appendix in the book serves one or more of the following key purposes:

1. To provide more detailed, supplemental information on certain topics;
2. To provide guidance for more extensive project work;
3. To allow easy access to certain basic information necessary to proceed with term-long projects;
4. To provide "refresher-type" information on topics to which the reader may not have had recent exposure.

Key Terms / Glossary

Key terms are highlighted in bold print when first used. A listing of key terms is provided at the end of each chapter to help the reader identify and confirm understanding of the terminology of financial information. Appendix H: Glossary provides working definitions for these terms.

Changes in this Second Edition

A thorough review by the author and helpful comments, suggestions, and recommendations from faculty, students, and other reviewers prompted several changes to the initial edition of this text.

- Modifications to improve readability have been made.
- Updates of time sensitive financial statistics are provided.
- Recent changes to the consumer price index are reviewed.
- An alternate term project has been developed and included.
- The introduction of the new Euroland currency (the "Euro") is discussed.
- The timing and scope of US currency changes are reviewed.
- Additional and revised review questions, exercises, and cases/problems for several chapters have been developed and included.
- Internet web sites pertinent to the subject matter have been added at the end of many chapters.

Acknowledgments

Several individuals were instrumental in the conception, development, review, revision, and publishing of this book. From Northwood University Administration, I thank Dr. Robert Serum and Dean Timothy Nash for supporting the project. From Northwood University Academics, I thank fellow faculty members Elmer Tofteland and Otis Wilson for their ideas, support, comments, and use of the book. The support of present and past students of Northwood University was a beacon in my quest to finalize this book. Their input and insistence that a book like this be developed was an inspiration.

Most of all, I'd like to again thank my wonderful family, especially my wife Liz and son Thomas. Without them, life has little purpose.

About the Author

Mark J. Minbiole has a Master's degree in Business Administration, is a certified public accountant, and is licensed as a certified financial planner. He has had over 20 years of financial management experience in such diverse areas as public accounting; corporate accounting and finance; commercial and investment banking; and university-level education, at the undergraduate and graduate levels. He also is founder, President, and CEO of Vector Enterprises, Inc., a corporation engaged in publishing, technical authorship, and financial consulting to individuals, corporations, and not-for-profit organizations.

PART ONE

FINANCIAL INFORMATION - BACKGROUND

"What financial information do I need to make this decision?"

Part One: Financial Information - Background begins the exploration of financial information by describing why financial information is important (Chapter 1) and identifying the myriad sources of financial information available (Chapter 2).

While not all decisions require the obtaining and interpreting of financial information, many do! The fields of economics, accounting, law, finance, banking, investments, and others each involve the investigative process of searching for financial information from various sources and then fully analyzing this information.

Chapter 1: Why is Financial Information So Important? clarifies why financial information is important by addressing such issues as:

- the differences between data and information
- uses of financial information
- key attributes of financial information.

Chapter 2: Sources of Financial Information uncovers the various sources of financial information, who develops the information, and who uses it by examining:

- the three key sectors of the United States economy
- the role of third-party financial information providers
- the recurring contents of *The Wall Street Journal.*

Chapter 1

Why is Financial Information Important?

Chapter Concepts

After mastering the material in this chapter, the reader will be able to:

- describe the differences between data and information
- describe the role of management in an enterprise
- identify personal uses of financial information
- understand the primary goal of a business person
- understand the primary financial goal of an individual
- describe the key attributes of information

Background

The role that financial information plays in today's global economy cannot be underestimated. Whether the individual is a businessperson or not, citizens are asked (or required) to be aware of the status of the economy, and to make good business, personal, economic or political decisions. The exercise of one's rights in a free market economy is enhanced by knowledge of such factors as:

- interest rates (short and long-term)
- employment statistics
- business cycle status
- stock market valuations
- bond market valuations
- current business topics
- how businesses are organized

As an example, as many businesses move away from fully providing lifelong employment and/or guaranteeing full pension / retirement benefits, workers find themselves in the position of ensuring the adequacy of their own financial future. One technique employed is the use of retirement savings plans, company-sponsored retirement plans, and/or individual investment accounts. Knowledge of some of the aforementioned factors is essential to effectively preparing for one's financial future.

The Importance of Financial Information

Data vs. Information

Data is the "fuel" that makes the decision "engine" go. But ***information*** makes that engine run smoothly and efficiently. Just as an oil refinery processes crude oil into more usable and valuable petroleum-based products, so does the processing of *data* "refine" it into *information* that is useful in decision making.

This is a very subtle yet important distinction between data and information. In its simplest expression, information is data that has value to the user. Often, data is the raw material, and information is work in process. The decision(s) made after careful review, interpretation, and analysis of the data is the ultimate goal of the decision-maker.

Role of Management

In a business setting, **management** uses information to fulfill its primary role: to find and fix problems to maximize the value of the company for the benefit of its shareholders/owners. Management needs good information to make those key decisions.

Personal Uses of Financial Information

In a similar fashion, individuals need information to make decisions. Consider the following questions an individual may be faced with:

- Which stock should I buy or sell?
- Are interest rates going up or down?
- Will this mutual fund continue to grow in value?
- How will the strength of the US dollar vis-à-vis the Japanese yen affect the purchase price of Japanese made goods?

See Exhibit 1.1 for an overview of the role of data and information in decision making.

Exhibit 1.1: Role of Data/Information in Decision Making

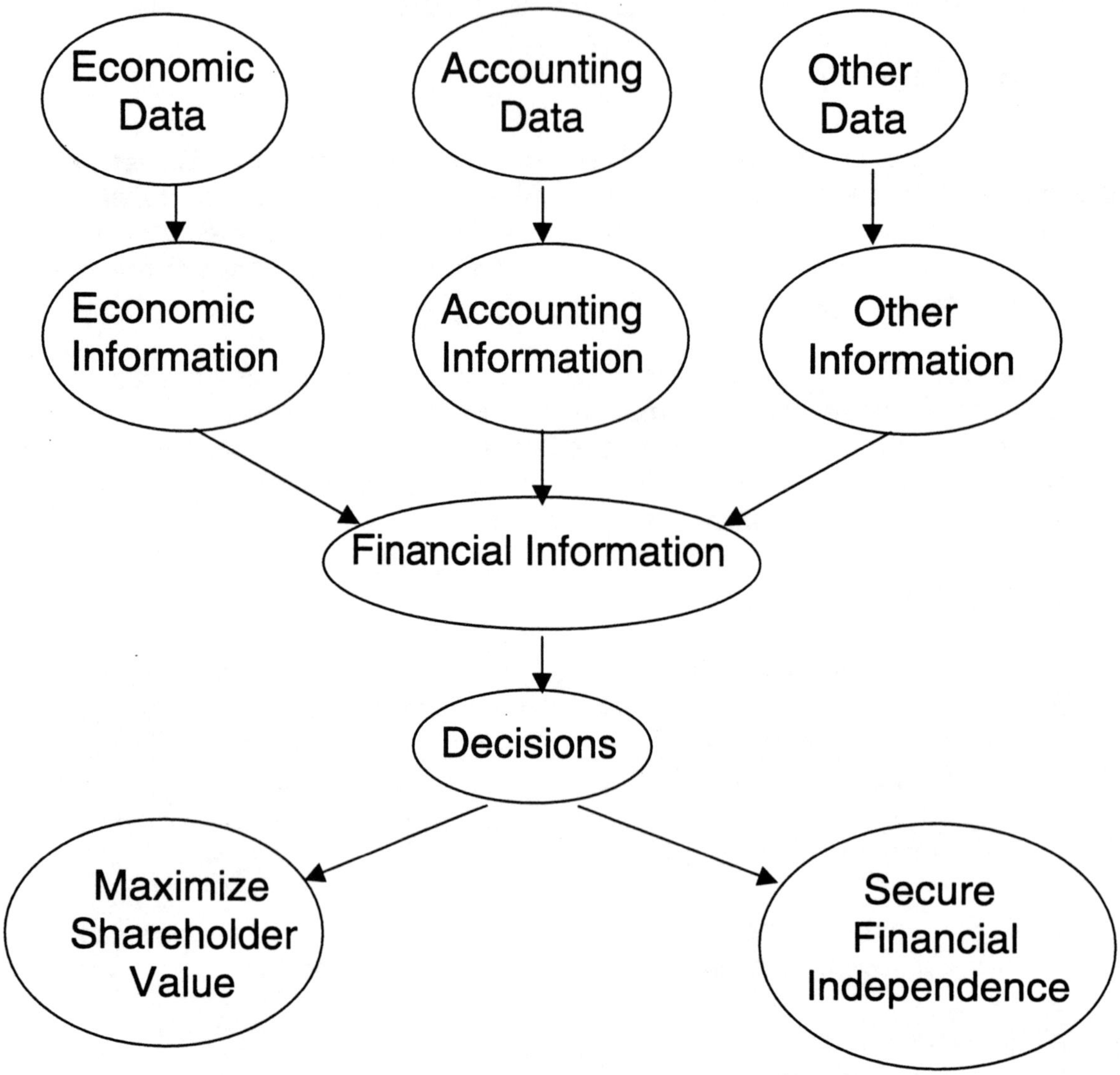

Individuals gather, sort, and prune pertinent economic, accounting, and other information to generate financial information useful to make decisions, having a significant goal in mind. The goal for a businessperson is to maximize shareholder value. The goal for an individual is to secure financial independence.

Information Attributes

Information is best when it meets the following criteria:

1. Timeliness: appropriate information is available before a decision must be made;
2. Reliability: the information can be counted upon to be reasonably accurate;
3. Relevance: having the information will result in better decision making.

See Exhibit 1.2.

Exhibit 1.2: Critical Information Attributes

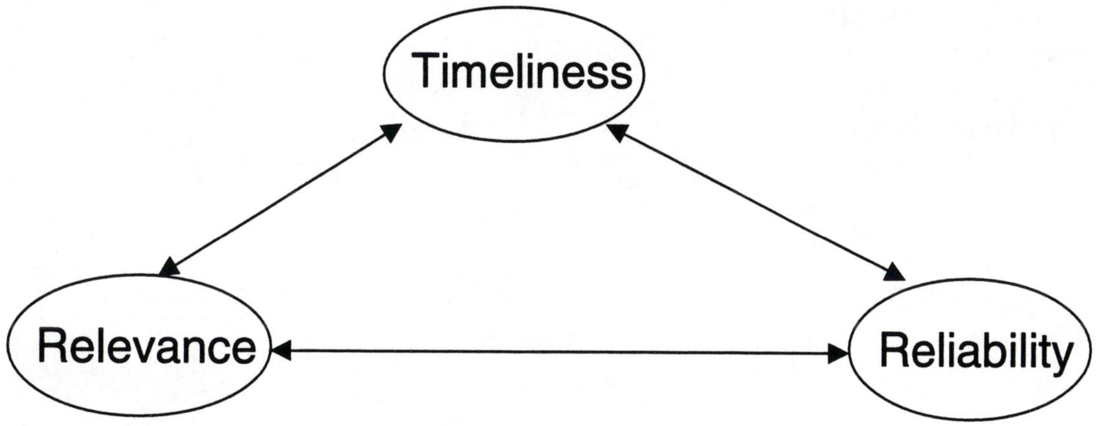

Maximize Shareholder Value

Business people are responsible for leading and managing the organization in an ethical and responsible manner. Their goal to "maximize shareholder value" or "maximize the value of the firm" means they must strive to make the organization as "valuable" as possible. For a for-profit corporation, the best "scorecard" for determining **shareholder value** is the stock price. Effectively using financial information is key to shareholder value maximization.

Secure Financial Independence

As described earlier, individuals are finding themselves more and more self-reliant for their financial future. Effectively using financial information is key to ensuring a healthy financial future for the individual.

Summary

The **free enterprise system** places ultimate responsibility on the individual to manage his/her own affairs; the government is a last resort. In order to fulfill this responsibility, individuals must master the ability to find, read, interpret, and analyze financial data.

Key Terms

data
free enterprise system
information
management
personal responsibility
shareholder value

Name Date Section

Problems/Cases

P1-1 Congratulations! You have won the lottery worth $1,000,000! What financial information would you like to have in order to make best use of the money?

Name **Date** **Section**

P1-2 Read Appendix A and complete the research assignment analyzing interest rates paid by local financial institutions on consumer deposits.

Materials for Further Reference

Chilton, David. *The Wealthy Barber.* Rocklin, CA: Prima Publishing, 1993.

Rothchild, John. *A Fool and His Money.* New York: John Wiley & Sons, 1998

Tobias, Andrew. *The Only Investment Guide You'll Ever Need.* Harvest Books, 1999.

Tyson, Eric. *Personal Finance for Dummies.* Foster City, CA: IDG Books Worldwide, 1996.

Internet Web Sites to Explore

www.troweprice.com

www.vanguard.com

Chapter 2

Sources of Financial Information

Chapter Concepts

After mastering the material in this chapter, the reader will be able to:

- identify the three key sectors of the United States economy
- identify the role of third-party information providers
- identify examples of financial information sources as well as their respective users and providers
- identify key categories of financial information sources within the "third-party information provider" group
- identify the three key sections of *The Wall Street Journal* and their respective contents

Background

The United States is said to have a three-sector economy, consisting of Businesses, Governments, and Households. See Exhibit 2.1. The interdependence among these three sectors necessitates a tremendous flow of information to improve decision making by each sector. While there are various classifications of information, we will focus on financial information, which might present itself, for example, as economic, accounting, fiscal, monetary, or investment information.

Each sector of the USA economy both provides and uses information. The information provided by each respective sector is used not only by that sector but often by the other two sectors as well. This chapter focuses on the numerous, available sources of financial information. Later chapters focus on uses and interpretation of this information.

Exhibit 2.1: The Three Sector USA Economy

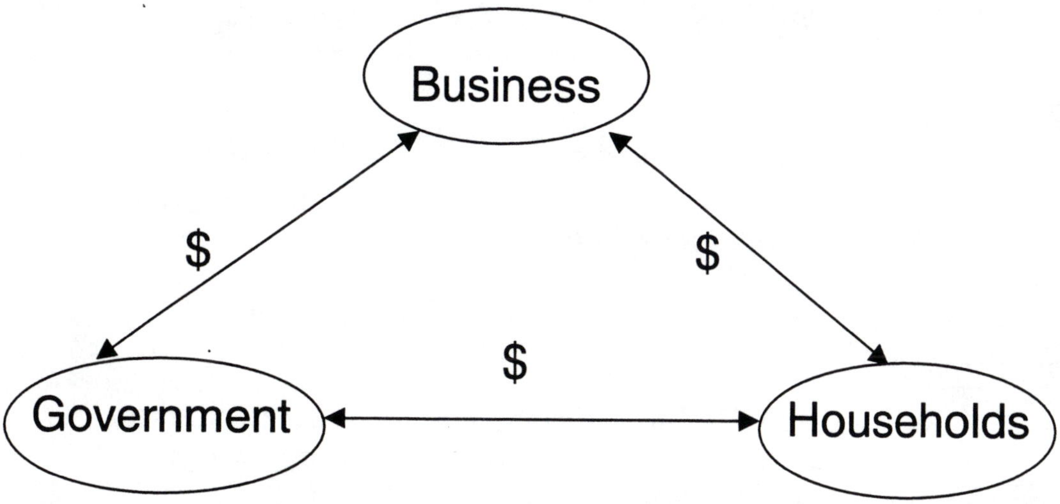

Financial Information Sources

The Three Sector USA Economy

As described in Chapter 1, information is what makes the decision engine run. The free flow of information maximizes the potential effectiveness and efficiency of the decision making process.

Each of the three sectors (Business, Government, and Households) provides certain data and desires certain information. With respect to financial information, see Exhibit 2.2 for examples of data/information provided and desired by each of the three sectors.

Exhibit 2.2: Examples of Financial Data by Sector

	Desires	*Provides*
Households:	economic data fiscal data financial reports	income tax data demographics
Government:	income tax data business operations data demographic data	economic data census data
Business:	economic data fiscal data demographic data operations data	financial reports income tax data

In addition to these three key players is a group of "**third-party information**" providers that are also involved in providing and using data/information. This group forms an industry whose mission is to obtain data and "package" it (often with analytical commentary) for use by others, often for a fee.

The Information Industry

Examples of groups within this industry are "traditional" media (e.g. radio, television, newspapers, magazines, etc.); "non-traditional" media (e.g. **Internet** service providers, etc.); advisory services (e.g. *Dun & Bradstreet, Value Line, Morningstar,* etc.); and data repackagers (e.g. Ibbottson & Associates, trade associations, etc.)

We will consider the information industry to be an additional member of the three-sector economy for the purposes of our search and interpretation of financial information sources. See Exhibit 2.3. We will call this sector: "Third-Party Information Providers".

Exhibit 2.3: Providers and Users of Financial Information

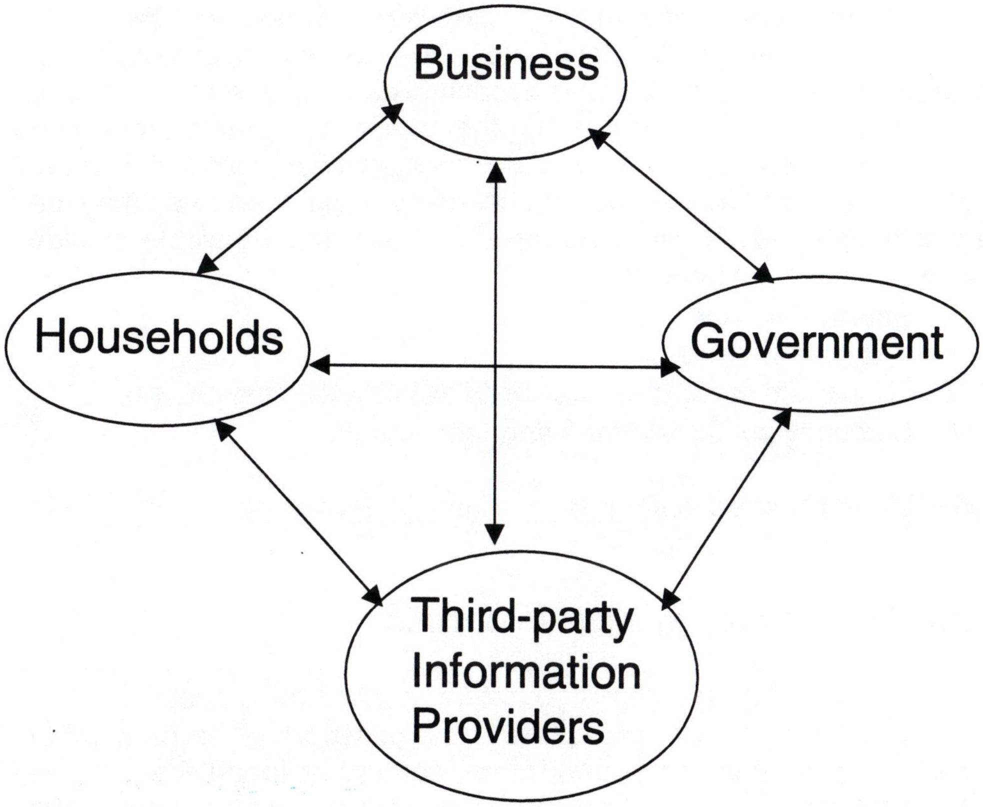

Note: Relatively new to some individuals is the power of the expanding universe of valuable information on the Internet. With a personal computer, phone hook-up, Internet access, and dedicated software, individuals can perform intricate and complicated financial information searches. Everything from Wall Street research reports, to stock quotes, to foreign exchange rates, to Federal Reserve Chairman speech texts, to who-knows-what is at the fingertips of an experienced "Net navigator".

The exploding number of financial activities include banking on-line, mutual fund searching, stock and bond transactions, and personal financial projection software.

Chances are the Internet will become an even more important player in financial information in the near future. Note; a sample of relevant web sites is listed at the end of each chapter.

Business Sources of Financial Information

Businesses are prodigious providers and users of data/information. Businesses generate enormous amounts of data/information from each aspect of the company: accounting, planning, marketing, research, operations, customer service, logistics, etc. The key sources of financial data consist primarily of accounting and economic data. Some of this data is highly confidential and is used only within the company. Examples include most compensation data, much legal data, product line profitability, trade secrets, etc. Other information, by choice or by legal mandate, may be available outside the publicly owned company. Information available outside the company includes the following:

- **Annual Reports**
- **Proxy Statements**
- Filings with the **Securities and Exchange Commission**
- Company public relations announcements

These items will be explored in Chapter 5: Financial Reporting.

Government Sources of Financial Information

Anyone who has filled out an income tax return, applied for a social security number, obtained a driver's license, applied for a passport, or had any other dealings with the government (federal, state, county, or local) realizes the tremendous amount of information/data the government requests and obtains. But does the government share any of that information? You bet!

Let's look briefly at the federal government and its role as a provider of information. Whether it is an **inflation** index, a report of **leading economic indicators**, international trade balances, census data, **unemployment** rates, or the **federal deficit**, we are exposed to government-provided information. While households, businesses, and governmental units provide enormous amounts of data/information to the federal government, the federal government "refines" much of that data and generates information for businesses, households, and governmental units to use. Chapter 3 looks at various sources of government information including economic data, forecasting data, and fundamental market data (such as interest rates).

Household Sources of Financial Information

Most household or "consumer" data, if shared at all, is most apt to be shared with businesses or governmental units rather than with other consumers. Data such as income, household inhabitants, etc. are likely to be shared with the government (by law!) through the filing of income tax returns, filling out census data requests, etc.

Businesses collect data from households also. Beyond the basic transaction data that arises from an item purchase (e.g. credit card number, item description, serial number, name, address, phone number, etc.), a business may also ask for information about the purchaser and his/her family, as through the use of a questionnaire on a warranty card. Data such as household income, number of family members, why they bought the product, key hobbies, etc. may be requested. Businesses may go beyond this collection process to soliciting information via opinion polls and focus groups.

Usually, where customers are the key providers of data/information, such data is analyzed and organized by others before it is deemed useful.

Third Party Financial Information Sources

Thousands of companies exist for the sole purpose of "refining" data into information. In fact, isn't that what the media is (supposedly) all about? Don't they (or shouldn't they) research facts, ideas, opinion, etc. and report their findings?

Exhibit 2.4 shows just a sampling of the financial information "products" of these providers.

In this book, we will focus on *The Wall Street Journal*, but we will access several other sources for our study.

Exhibit 2.4: Examples of Key Information Sources Produced by Third-Party Providers

Television

CNBC
CNNFN
Nightly Business Review
Wall Street Week

Newspapers

Barron's
Financial Times
Investors' Business Daily
The Wall Street Journal

Magazines

Business Week
Forbes
Fortune
Kiplinger's
Money
Mutual Funds
Smart Money
Worth

Advisory Services

Dun & Bradstreet
Ibbottson & Associates
Moody's
Morningstar
Robert Morris & Associates
Standard & Poors
TRW
Value Line

Internet

Alta Vista
America Online
Excite
Prodigy
Yahoo

Books

classics
current topics
textbooks

The Wall Street Journal

To many individuals, *The Wall Street Journal* is the daily business bible. Launched originally as a two-page letter by Charles H. Dow and Edward Jones in 1882 as the *Customers' Afternoon Letter*, it took on its present name in 1889.

The Wall Street Journal has evolved considerably over its 100-year history. According to Paul Steiger, its current managing editor, "Our mission is to be in touch with the markets, with the economy, and with companies and industries and how they perform, compete, and interact."

Published each business day, *The Wall Street Journal* is typically printed in three sections:

The *first section* reports on the most important breaking news stories of the day that affect business, including economic reports and important corporate announcements and changes.

The *second section* is called "Marketplace". It focuses on news of how companies set strategies to compete, changes in consumers, and how new technologies and other factors are affecting the way we work and sell.

The *third section* is called "Money & Investing" and is a comprehensive guide to investment news and statistics from USA and foreign markets.

Much of the remainder of this book delves into the interpretation of information presented in *The Wall Street Journal.* We will find that much of the financial information useful to decision makers that is provided by government and business is effectively summarized and analyzed in *The Wall Street Journal.*

Supplemental Readings

- *The Wall Street Journal*
- *The Wall Street Journal Educational Issue: How To Read Between The Lines*
- *The Wall Street Journal* video

Summary

The number of sources of financial information is enormous. By categorizing these sources into "Business", "Government", and "Third Parties", we can more effectively compare, contrast, and interpret these sources more effectively. Our focus will be as follows:

Sector	Data/Information	Chapter(s)
• Government	Key economic statistics	3
• Business	Annual Reports	5
• Third Parties	*The Wall Street Journal*	6 - 9, 11,12

Key Terms

annual report
federal deficit
inflation
Internet
leading economic indicators
Proxy statement
SEC forms:
- Form 8-K
- Form 10-K
- Form 10-Q

Securities and Exchange Commission
trade deficit
third-party information provider
unemployment

Name **Date** **Section**

E2-2 Locate and describe an Internet web site that is a significant source of financial information.

Name | Date | Section

Problems/Cases

P2-1 How will the expansion of the Internet affect financial information?

Name ______________________ Date __________ Section ______

P2-2 Who is responsible for the timeliness, reliability, and relevance of financial information?

Materials for Further Reference

Mayo, Herbert. *Investments: An Introduction: Fifth Edition.* Ft. Worth, TX: Dryden Press, 1997.

Stull, Andrew T. *Surfing for Success in Business: A Student's Guide to the Internet.* Englewood Cliffs, NJ: Prentice Hall, 1997.

See also list of third party information providers in Exhibit 2.4.

Internet Web Sites to Explore

www.cnnfn.com

www.excite.com

www.paulmerriman.com

www.usatoday.com

www.yahoo.com

PART TWO

FINANCIAL INFORMATION - GOVERNMENT SOURCES

The government is a key part of our three-sector economy in the US. Chapter 3: Government Information, the sole chapter in Part Two: Financial Information - Government Sources, describes how the government (primarily the Federal government) plays a key role in accumulating data and publishing financial information about:

- recent economic activity, to determine the extent of growth or decline;
- changes in consumer prices, to determine the rate of "inflation";
- other key variables in the economy, particularly ones that tend to be good predictors of future economic activity.

Part Two: Financial Information - Government Sources explores each of these crucial areas in detail. Chapter 3 explains the importance of GDP (Gross Domestic Product), the final output of all goods and services produced in the United States. The chapter also delves into CPI (Consumer Price Index), which reflects the change in the prices of consumer goods from one year to the next. Finally, the eleven "Leading Economic Indicators" are reviewed, in the context of their relative importance in predicting the near-term direction of the economy.

Chapter 3

Government Information

Chapter Concepts

After mastering the material in this chapter, the reader will be able to:

- describe Gross Domestic Product and each of its major components
- explain the purpose, uses, and foibles of the Consumer Price Index
- recognize the Leading Economic Indicators and their use in predicting future economic conditions

Background

In Chapter 2: Sources of Financial Information, we learned that the government is one of the three key players in our multi-sector economy. See Exhibit 3.1.

As such, the government acts as a huge repository of information as it collects data from businesses, households, and various government agencies. The goal of such data collection is to help the government make better decisions once the collected data is analyzed. Much of this information is made available to households and businesses, so *they* can make better decisions as well.

We will focus on three key areas of government information that relate directly to the economy and finance: GDP (Gross Domestic Product), CPI (Consumer Price Index), and LEI (Leading Economic Indicators). Other important government information (e.g. money supply, Federal Reserve actions, interest rates, etc.) are covered elsewhere in this book.

Exhibit 3.1: The Three Sector USA Economy

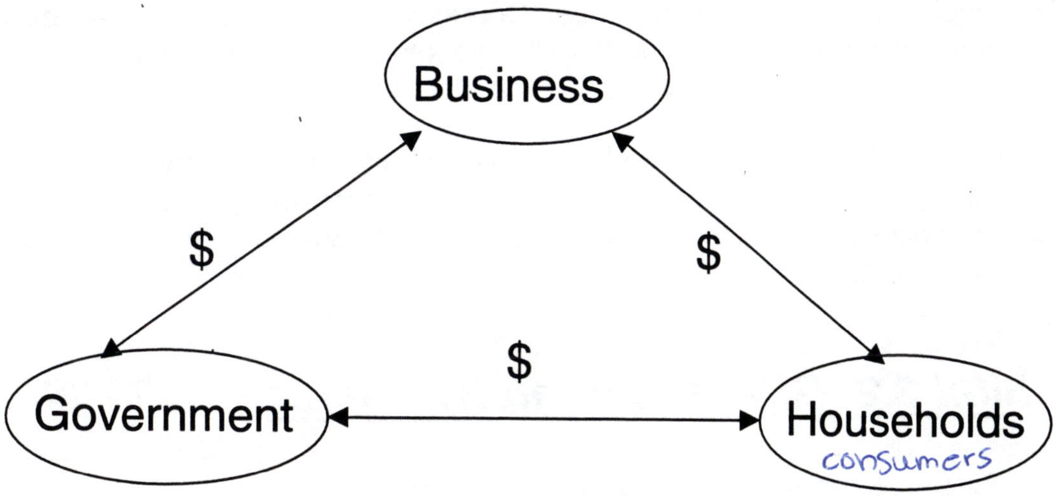

GDP: Gross Domestic Product

GDP (Gross Domestic Product) is the broadest available measure of "output" economic activity in the United States. It provides the official scale to measure changes in economic activity, in terms of final output expenditures.

Quoted quarterly in terms of an annual percentage change from the previous quarter, it focuses on the following key *spending* components of the USA economy:

- ***C***onsumption (consumers)
- ***I***nvestment
    - non-residential (business) "capital"
    - residential house, land (households) "newly built"
    - inventory change (business)
- ***G***overnment
- E***x***ports
- I***m***ports

GDP = C+I+G+(X−m)

Algebraically, GDP is determined as follows:

$GDP = C + I + G + (X - M)$	Formula 3-1

This formula says the following: "Gross Domestic Product is the sum of the four key expenditure categories in the US economy. Personal Consumption plus Investment plus Government Spending plus Net Exports equals GDP."

Note that "Net Exports" consists of total exports minus total imports. Conceptually, GDP is calculated by adding together the spending of the three key sectors of the United States economy, as shown in the following chart: Exhibit 3.2.

Exhibit 3.2: GDP Spending By Sector

	C	I	G	X	M
Business	X	X		X	X
Government			X		
Households	X	X	_	X	X
Total	X	X	X	X	X

C = Consumption

I = Investment

G = Government spending

X = Exports

M = Imports

Let's take a look at each GDP component separately.

C = Personal ***C***onsumption

Personal **consumption** expenditures measure purchases of food, clothing, shelter, services, vehicles, and other durable goods such as household furniture and appliances.

I = ***I***nvestment

Investment expenditures' three sub-components are included as follows:

Non-residential investment + residential investment + inventory change

> ***Non-residential investment*** refers to the machinery, equipment, factories, warehouses, offices and retail and wholesale establishments purchased by business during the quarter.
>
> ***Residential investment*** is the amount spent by consumers on the purchase of newly built homes during the quarter. These expenditures are included in "***I***" (***I***nvestment) rather than "***C***" (Personal ***C***onsumption) because of the more long-lasting character of the items purchased.
>
> ***Inventory change*** measures the net increase in businesses' stocks of goods during the quarter. In other words, when business inventories go up, expenditures have been made to build the inventory, but the *final* sale has yet to take place. However, GDP measures *final output*, not final sale. Therefore, an increase in inventory counts as additional investment, while a decrease in inventory counts as a deduction.

G = ***G***overnment Spending

> ***G*overnment spending** accounts for expenditures of all governmental units: federal, state, and local municipalities, including dollars spent on salaries and purchases of goods and services (e.g. military hardware) and public works and structures (such as roads, bridges, and public buildings). It does not include transfer payments such as Social Security benefits.

X - M = Net Exports

Net export spending reflects the difference between:

1. **Exports**: the money *received* for goods and services produced/provided in the United States and shipped outside its boundaries; and
2. **Imports**: the money *paid* for goods and services provided from outside the United States.

Note: this number (***X - M***) could be negative, indicating imports exceeded exports. This imbalance is known as a **trade deficit** to the United States, a situation the country has been in vis-à-vis the rest of the world for 25 years!

To obtain summarized GDP data, one need only look to *The Wall Street Journal* (See Appendix G). *The Wall Street Journal* provides GDP data and analyses on a regular basis, typically in a statistical summary format. This format describes GDP using the aforementioned format/formula: GDP = C + I + G + (X - M) . The numbers plus expert commentary provide the reader with a good overview of the status of the United States economy.

Impact of Inflation

Consider the following example: the cost of a specific automobile goes from $20,000 one year to $21,000 the next year, a 5% increase. Assuming an equal number of these automobiles was sold each of the two years, total spending on these goods increased the same 5%. Did economic activity *really* increase? NO! Only the cost increased. To eliminate the impact of changing prices, the government calculates GDP using two methods:

*Current-dollar or **Nominal GDP*** measures actual changes in *dollar spending*, including the impact of changing prices.

*Constant-dollar or **Real GDP*** measures actual changes in *output*, eliminating the impact of "inflation". (Inflation measures the impact of price changes on similar goods/services from year to year.)

Unless there is a specific mention to the contrary, GDP figures reflect *real* activity, i.e. with inflation removed. This adjustment allows for data to be interpreted and analyzed without the impact of changing prices. Therefore, changes in GDP reflect changes in the *volume* of goods and services, a more meaningful comparison in most cases.

CPI: Consumer Price Index

We will discuss the CPI in greater detail in Chapter 6, but an introduction now to this key economic statistic is important. Think of the **CPI** as measuring the change in prices from one year to the next of a market basket full of representative goods and services that Americans buy. Key components of the CPI are:

- housing
- food
- transportation
- medical care
- clothing
- entertainment
- other services

disinflation: when rate of inflation slows down

Since 1967, inflation (as measured by the CPI) has been as high as 13.5% (1980) and as low as 1.2% (1986). These percentages reflect the numerical percentage change in that market basket of goods and services. It does *not* imply that *every* item changed by that amount. It merely indicates that as a whole, prices changed by that amount. Indeed, some prices may have gone down, even when the overall percentage reflects an increase!

Consternation over the precise accuracy of the CPI does exist, although recent changes are designed to address those concerns. Starting in January 1999, the Bureau of Labor Statistics (BLS) will use a new formula, called a geometric mean estimator, to calculate the price changes for several categories in the CPI. This formula takes into account the fact that consumers typically respond to higher prices by making substitutions in their purchases. The BLS estimates that the new formula will reduce the CPI by .2% per year. The categories that will not use the new formula include certain housing, utility, and medical costs.

Additionally, the Bureau of Labor Statistics has indicated that it will update the consumption expenditure weights in the CPI every two years instead of once per decade as is now done, beginning in January 2002. A more timely and flexible measure of consumer spending patterns is expected to give a more accurate picture of inflation in the US economy. The weights will replace the 1993-95 weights and reflect prices of the 1999-2000 period. Another change reflected in the new plan envisions expenditure weights never being more than four years old.

LEI: Leading Economic Indicators

Economists have devised a set of statistics to help explain economic activity. These "indicators" tend to move up or down ahead of GDP, making these indicators valuable for their predictive capabilities. They are known as the Leading Economic Indicators.

While no one has a perfect crystal ball, these indicators provide valuable data to economists and others who are trying to predict the next move in the **business cycle** (the general direction of the economy): up ("**boom**") or down ("**bust**"). What information do you think the Chief Executive Officer of a major corporation would like to have before approving a significant expansion of capacity? Don't you think s/he would like to get the best forward looking data possible? Is a **recession** looming? If so, s/he might want to hold off expansion plans.

What are these leading economic indicators? This composite index is made up of the eleven key components identified in Exhibit 3.3.

Exhibit 3.3: Leading Economic Indicators

1. *Average weekly hours* of production for non-supervisory workers, manufacturing

2. Average weekly *initial claims for unemployment* insurance, state programs

3. *Manufacturers' new orders* in 1982 dollars, consumer goods and materials industries

4. *Vendor performance* - slower deliveries diffusion index

5. Contract and *orders for plant and equipment* in 1982 dollars

6. *New private housing units* authorized by local building permits

7. *Change in manufacturers' unfilled orders* in 1982 dollars, durable goods industries

8. Change in sensitive *materials prices*

9. *Stock prices*, 500 common stocks

10. *Money supply* - M2 - in 1982 dollars

11. Index of *consumer expectations*

While many indicators in the economy are valuable, these eleven are especially "anointed" due to their critical attributes, as follows:

- accurately leads the business cycle
- provides comprehensive coverage of the various aspects of the United States economy
- timely availability on a frequent basis with high reliability

For some of these indicators (i.e., 1,3,4,5,6,7,9,10,11), an increase represents a positive outlook and anticipation of good economic times. For the other indicators (i.e., 2,8), an increase represents a negative outlook, anticipation of worsening economic times. Note: many of these indicators are more fully explored in Chapter 6: Money.

Supplemental Reading

- Appendix G

Summary

Government information plays a crucial role in the decision-making processes of businesses, households, and governmental units themselves. While most of the data is provided to the government, their ability to sort, analyze, report, and interpret the data is invaluable. Although the government provides enormous amounts of data and information, we have focused on three key areas: Gross Domestic Product, Consumer Price Index, and Leading Economic Indicators. Taken together, these three sources are instrumental in evaluating the status of the economy, changing prices, and where the economy may be headed.

Key Terms

boom
business cycle
bust
CPI
Consumption
Exports
GDP
Government spending
Imports
inventory change
Investment
LEI
Nominal GDP
non-residential investment
Real GDP
recession
residential investment

Name **Date** **Section**

E3-2 From **your** copy of *The Wall Street Journal*, cut out the most recent CPI article and tape it below. Summarize in your own words what the article says.

Name **Date** **Section**

E3-3 From **your** copy of *The Wall Street Journal*, cut out the most recent LEI article and tape it below. Summarize in your own words what the article says.

Name	Date	Section

Problems/Cases

P3-1 For each of the Leading Economic Indicators, indicate the current figure and whether it presages a boom (an economic upturn), a bust (an economic downturn / recession), or continuation of the current economic situation.

	Current Figure	Boom? Bust? Continuation?	
1.	______	______________	Average weekly hours of production for non-supervisory workers, manufacturing
2.	______	______________	Average weekly initial claims for unemployment insurance, state programs
3.	______	______________	Manufacturers' new orders in 1982 dollars, consumer goods and materials industries
4.	______	______________	Vendor performance - slower deliveries diffusion index
5.	______	______________	Contract and orders for plant and equipment in 1982 dollars
6.	______	______________	New private housing units authorized by local building permits
7.	______	______________	Change in manufacturers' unfilled orders in 1982 dollars, durable goods industries
8.	______	______________	Change in sensitive materials prices
9.	______	______________	Stock prices, 500 common stocks
10.	______	______________	Money supply - M2 - in 1982 dollars
11.	______	______________	Index of consumer expectations

Materials for Further Reference

Lehmann, Michael B. *The Irwin Guide to Using The Wall Street Journal*, 5th edition. Chicago, IL: Irwin Professional Publishing, 1996.

Lehmann, Michael B. *The Wall Street Journal Workbook*, 5th edition. Chicago, IL: Irwin, 1996.

Federal Reserve. *The Beige Book.*

Internet Web Sites to Explore

www.bls.gov

www.publicdebt.treas.gov/of/ofntebnd.htm

www.wsj.com

www.census.gov

PART THREE

FINANCIAL INFORMATION - BUSINESS SOURCES

In order to appreciate the significance of business sources of financial information in the decision making process, we must examine two key areas: 1. The various forms of business organization; and 2. Financial reporting. Part Three: Financial Information - Business Sources will be our guide.

Chapter 4: Forms of Business Organization explores the three primary forms of business organization and key attributes of each. Newer, hybrid forms of business organization are also discussed.

Chapter 5: Financial Reporting explores the sources of financial information that publicly owned businesses must disclose, by focusing on Annual Reports.

Chapter 4

Forms of Business Organization

Chapter Concepts

After mastering the material in this chapter, the reader will be able to:

- describe the three primary forms of business organization
- identify the key attributes of each of the three primary forms of business organization
- identify the unique advantages of the newer hybrid forms of business organization

Background

The second most important decision when starting up a company is the legal "form" the organization will take. (The most important decision is probably what products or services will be provided!) The business organization form decision has significant legal, financial, tax, and accounting consequences. An inappropriate choice may prove to be very costly.

There are three basic forms of business organization: the sole proprietorship, the partnership, and the corporation. While other, less common forms exist, they are typically "hybrid" forms of business organization, with their basic structure following the format of one of the three basic forms, but then adding characteristics of one or both of the other forms. Examples include "S" Corporations, limited liability companies, and limited liability partnerships.

Five key defining characteristics exist for each of the forms of business:
- number of owners
- transferability of interests
- taxation
- liability
- legal formation papers

Additionally, each form of business has several advantages and disadvantages vis-à-vis the alternative forms. Other defining characteristics for each form of business organization are also discussed.

The Three Basic Forms of Business

Sole Proprietorship

Statistics indicate that approximately 75% of the 21 million business firms in the US use the **sole proprietorship** form. However, even though sole proprietorships account for the vast majority of companies, this business form accounts for only about 6% of the revenues. In other words, most businesses use the sole proprietorship business form, but in total produce little of the revenues of business in the USA. The key, defining feature of a sole proprietorship is the fact that there is one and only one owner. Even still, sole proprietorships account for about 27% of the company profits in the USA!

Sole proprietorships do not pay taxes. That obligation is the responsibility of the owner of the business, not the business itself. It is the owner's responsibility to ensure that all appropriate taxes are paid. Typically, that is done by attaching a "Business Income" form ("Schedule C" from the Internal Revenue Service) to his/her individual tax return: Form 1040. In other words, the owner of a sole proprietorship includes the profits or losses from his/her business ventures with his/her non-business financial activities in calculating the required federal income taxes due.

The "sole proprietor", the individual who owns a sole proprietorship, takes full responsibility for the legal obligations of the company. This responsibility extends to his/her personal assets! Therefore, if the sole proprietorship is sued for any reason, and loses, it is the sole proprietor's obligation to make restitution, even if it involves going beyond the assets of the company and dipping into his/her own personal holdings, cash, investments, etc. As we will see, this is a definite disadvantage to opting for this form of business organization.

It is easy, inexpensive, and quick to set up a sole proprietorship. Often all that is needed is a trip to the local county offices to fill out a simple form and the payment of a nominal amount, maybe as low as $10. The form asks what the purpose of the business is and what the name of the company will be. After the county office clerk verifies that the company name chosen does not conflict with other names of companies in the county, approval to commence business can be granted.

The sole proprietorship is a popular form of business for several reasons. Because there is only one owner, decision making should be easier. Low set-up costs and low ongoing organization costs are also key benefits. However, the fact that the activities of the company are not legally separated from the individual owner from a liability perspective should cause the prospective business owner to consider the ramifications of this key disadvantage carefully before concluding that the sole proprietorship is the most appropriate form of business for him/her.

Partnership

If two or more individuals wish to join together to form a business organization, a **partnership** is one option available to them. They are precluded from establishing a sole proprietorship because that form of business organization limits the number of owners to one and only one. A partnership, however, is more flexible in this regard. A partnership can have as few as two owners or, theoretically, an infinite number! Practically speaking, except in unusual circumstances, partnerships rarely have more that 30-50 owners, called "partners". Partnerships account for a small percentage of the firms in the USA, approximately 6%, 4%, and 3% of the number of firms, total revenues, and total profits, respectively.

Like sole proprietorships, partnerships do not pay taxes. That obligation is the responsibility of the owners ("partners") of the business. It is their responsibility to ensure that all appropriate taxes are paid, typically in "**prorata form**". "Prorata form" means that the partners must decide when they form the partnership how any losses or profits will be shared or distributed among the partners. That determination is used to allocate the profits (or losses) of the partnership each year for each partner to pay appropriate taxes. Typically, a "Schedule K-1" is prepared by the partnership for each partner to formally acknowledge the partner's share of the partnership's profits or losses. This is in addition to an informational tax return form (IRS Form 1065) filed with the IRS directly. This IRS tax schedule is used in preparing the partner's individual tax return - Form 1040. In other words, each partner of a partnership includes his/her prorata share of the profits or losses from the partnership's business ventures with his/her non-business financial activities in calculating the required federal income taxes due.

Each partner takes full responsibility for the legal obligations of the company. Note that this responsibility extends beyond the actions any individual partner takes. Each partner is responsible for each of the business actions of every partner! And this responsibility extends to his/her personal assets! Therefore, if the partnership is sued for any reason, and loses, each partner maybe held liable individually. It is the partnership's obligation to make restitution, even if it involves going beyond the assets of the company and dipping into individual partner's own personal holdings, cash, investments, etc. As in the case of the sole proprietorship, this is a definite disadvantage to opting for this form of business organization.

It is relatively easy, inexpensive, and quick to set up a partnership. Because a partnership by definition will have more than one owner, some prearrangement must be made to determine how any profits and/or losses will be distributed to each individual partner. The prearrangement papers are known as Articles of Partnership. The papers clearly spell out such matters as loss sharing, profit sharing, management responsibilities, place of business, business name, etc. All partners must sign the Articles of Partnership, indicating that they agree to abide by these "bylaws". After the development of the Articles of Partnership, often all that is needed is a trip to the local county offices to fill out a simple form and the payment of a nominal amount, maybe as low as $10. The form asks what the purpose of the business is and what the name of the company will be. After the county office clerk verifies that the company name chosen does not conflict with other names of companies in the county, approval to commence business can be granted.

Transfer of ownership in a partnership is not easily accomplished. Generally speaking, whenever a partner leaves the partnership or an individual is admitted to the partnership, a new partnership must be created. Although perhaps transparent outside the partnership, much legal and administrative work may be necessary to accomplish this transition.

The partnership may be the appropriate popular form of business in a particular situation for several reasons. Other than initially drafting the Articles of Partnership and the ongoing requirement to prepare the "Schedule K-1", set up costs and ongoing organization costs are low. However, the fact that the activities of the partnership are not legally separated from the individual partners from a liability perspective should cause the prospective business owners to consider the ramifications of this key disadvantage carefully before concluding that the partnership is the most appropriate form of business for them.

Corporation

If one or more individuals wish to form a business organization, the **corporation** is one option available to them. Unlike a partnership, a corporation can have just one owner. Unlike a sole proprietorship, a corporation can have more than one owner. Therefore, a corporation may have as few as one owner or an infinite number! Corporations account for a modest percentage of the firms in the USA, accounting for approximately 19% of the number of firms. However, when it comes to measuring which form of business "produces" the vast majority of revenues and profits in the

USA, the corporate form of business organization accounts for approximately 90% and 70%, respectively!

Unlike sole proprietorships and partnerships, corporations DO pay taxes. States recognize corporations as "persons" and as such corporations are required to pay federal and state taxes. Owners are known as shareholders, stockholders, or share owners. Unlike sole proprietorships and partnerships, the obligation to pay taxes on business operations is NOT the responsibility of the owners ("shareholders" or "stockholders") of the business. The corporation pays its federal income taxes based upon its preparation of Internal Revenue Service Form 1120. Only if dividends are received by the shareholder from the corporation is the "owner" responsible for taxes on activities of the corporation. In other words, if a shareholder receives a dividend from a company in which they are an owner, s/he will be responsible for federal income taxes on the "dividend income" resulting from the distribution. But note that the corporation has already paid taxes! This results in the concept of "corporate **double taxation**". It is not that the corporation gets taxed twice. The "double taxation" come from the fact that the corporation pays dividends AFTER paying federal income taxes, and that the dividend is treated as taxable income to the shareholder, in which case they must also pay taxes! This "double taxation" is clearly a drawback to the corporate form of business.

Unlike partnerships where each partner takes full responsibility for the legal obligations of the company, corporation owners ("shareholders") are NOT personally liable for the actions that take place in the corporation. This is obviously a significant advantage to corporate ownership vis-à-vis partnerships or sole proprietorships. It is the corporation's responsibility to meet its legal obligation. Shareholders have **limited liability**, as their risk is typically limited to the value of their stock investment only.

While it is relatively easy, inexpensive, and quick to set up a sole proprietorship or a partnership, such is not the case for a corporation. Because a corporation is treated as a "person" in the eyes of federal and state law, prearrangement papers, known as Articles of Incorporation, must be drawn up. The papers clearly spell out such matters as officer titles and responsibilities, place of business, business name, etc. Because states reserve the right to grant corporate status, a state must approve the application for corporate status. This is not a simple matter like setting up a sole proprietorship or a partnership. Additionally, due to the lengthy and complex nature of the Articles of Incorporation, typically an attorney will be involved in the drafting, reviewing, and filing of the Articles of Incorporation.

The corporation may be the appropriate form of business in a particular situation for several reasons. Perhaps the most important two reasons are flexibility in numbers of owners and limited liability of owners. As previously stated, a corporation may have any number of owners. Also, liability for actions by the corporation is limited to the corporation itself and does not typically extend to the shareholders. Another key feature of the corporate form of business is the **divisibility and transferability of ownership**. "Sharing" ownership in a corporation by allowing more owners is accomplished quite easily, with little fanfare or legal intervention required. Additionally, selling part or all of an ownership position in a publicly owned corporation may be accomplished as easily as calling a stock broker!

Beyond the initial drafting of the Articles of Incorporation, ongoing legal requirements can be substantial, costly, and complicated for the corporate form of business. Regular reports to local, state, and federal governmental units are often required. Also, there are strict financial reporting requirements to corporate shareholders.

Hybrids

Creativity in business knows few bounds. Attempts to take the best features of each of the three basic forms of business organization have resulted in the following "hybrid" forms of business:

"S" Corporations - This form of business is like the regular corporate form (which is also known as a **"C" Corporation**) of business in most respects: liability is limited, paperwork is substantial, and divisibility and transfer of ownership are fairly easily accomplished. The key drawback of the C Corporation, "double taxation", is eliminated with an **S Corporation**. An S Corporation is taxed as if it were a partnership, a substantial advantage! However, S Corporations are limited to only 75 shareholders.

LLP and LLC - **LLPs** (Limited Liability Partnerships) are a relatively new hybrid form of business. As the name implies, this form of business minimizes the key disadvantage of a regular partnership: unlimited liability of each partner for the business actions of partners. **LLCs** (Limited Liability Companies) are also new on the scene. LLCs function much like S Corporations, but with no upper limit on the number of owners. State rules recognizing and regulating LLCs and LLPs are still in the developmental stage. As such, it is hard to generalize on them at this time.

Summary

Each business must adopt a specific form of business. Key considerations that need to be addressed are the number of owners, form of taxation, legal requirements, liability status, and ease of ownership transfer. While the initial choice is no doubt important, the changing nature of a business may warrant a change in the form of business after a period of time.

Creativity in business is alive and well: mutations of the basic business forms continue to appear on the scene.

Key Terms

C corporation
corporation
divisibility of ownership
double taxation
LLC (limited liability company)
LLP (limited liability partnership)
limited liability
ownership transfer
partnership
prorata form
S corporation
sole proprietorship

Name Date Section

E4-2 Fill in the attached chart.

	Sole Proprietorship	Partnership	Corporation
Percent of firms			
Percent of revenues			
Percent of profits			
Number of owners			
Transferability of interests			
Taxation			
Liability			
Legal papers			
Pros/cons			

Name	Date	Section

Problems/Cases

P4-1 You have decided to open your own business: an automobile detailing shop. Choose a form of business organization and explain why that form is best. Also explain why other forms of business organization are not as good for your situation.

Materials for Further Reference

Block and Hirt. *Fundamentals of Financial Management*, Eighth Edition. Chicago, IL: Irwin, 1996.

Internet Web Sites to Explore

www.troweprice.com

Chapter 5

Financial Reporting

Chapter Concepts

After mastering the material in this chapter, the reader will be able to:

- identify the three major financial statements and the purpose of each
- identify the major sections of a corporate Annual Report
- describe the purpose of accounting rules
- discuss the purpose of an audit opinion
- interpret financial data presented in corporate Annual Reports

Background

Financial reporting is the process of telling interested parties (government, current investors, potential investors, management, etc.) about the financial position, results of operations, and cash flows of a business.

While there is some flexibility and management judgment in how this is done, the process is subject to the regulations and procedures developed by rule-making bodies such as the Securities and Exchange Commission (SEC), the Financial Accounting Standards Board (FASB), the Governmental Accounting Standards Board (GASB), and the American Institute of Certified Public Accountants (AICPA). The purpose of these organizations is to enhance the reliability, relevance, and timeliness of financial information.

The Need for Rules

"Foolish consistency is the hobgoblin of simple minds."

Most endeavors in life need rules to maintain order and fairness. Imagine a country without any driving laws!!

- Which side of the road do you drive on?
- How fast can you go?
- What do you do when you approach a four-way intersection without stop signs or traffic lights?

Imagine a sport with no rules!

- How is the winner determined?
- How many players are allowed on the field of play?
- What rules of disqualification exist?
- How is a great player distinguished from an average one?

The need for rules in financial reporting are every bit as important as rules in driving or in sports. In business, the "winner" sees a long-run increase in his/her company's stock price. Only if consistent rules are developed, understood, applied, and verified can there be fair competition.

Financial reporting rules set out to do just that. Through organizations such as the AICPA, FASB, GASB, SEC, etc., rules, procedures, and guidelines are established, monitored, and enforced to make for a level playing field for participants. This process provides financial information users with information that is consistent, reliable, timely, relevant, and consistent.

These rules, procedures, and guidelines are codified as **GAAP**: **Generally Accepted Accounting Principles.** The consistent application of GAAP provides the "fair presentation" of financial information that decision-makers need.

Company Financial Reports

Each company whose stock is traded in the market must regularly file several reports describing their activities. Investors typically focus on four key reports: Form 10-K, Form 10-Q, the Proxy Statement, and the Annual Report.

The Proxy Statement and Forms 10-K and 10-Q are requirements of the Securities and Exchange Commission, a federal government agency, whose primary responsibility is to ensure that investors receive adequate information about publicly traded companies.

The **Form 10-K** is filed once each year, typically within three months after the company's year-end. The SEC stipulates a great deal of the content of the Form 10-K, including the following key items:

- Business
- Properties
- Legal Proceedings
- Submission of Matters to a Vote of Security Holders
- Executive Officers
- Market for Registrant's Common Equity and Related Stockholder Matters
- Changes in and Disagreements with Accountants on Accounting and Financial Disclosure
- Exhibits, Financial Statement Schedules, and Reports on Form 8-K

The **Form 10-Q**, a quarterly report, is also mandated by the SEC. However, while it is *much* abbreviated compared to the Form 10-K, Form 10-Q comes out on a quarterly basis, giving investors updated financial information on a company every three months.

The **Proxy Statement** is a communication device used by management of a company to formally solicit input from the company's shareholders. This input comes in the form of a voting ballot called a proxy. Along with some detailed information about the company, its board members, officers and compensation, and stock performance, the Proxy Statement puts before the stockholders issues of key importance. Such issues may include:

- nominations of board members
- appointment of independent accountants
- changes of management bonus plans
- changes in the number of authorized shares of stock

Shareholders, if they can garner enough support from fellow shareholders, are also entitled to include issues in the Proxy Statement, for a full vote of the shareholders. Shareholders vote on the proxy ballot in one of two ways:

1. They can indicate their preference on issue(s).
2. They can defer to management's judgment, allowing management to vote on their behalf in whatever manner management deems appropriate.

The Annual Report

The most widely available, read, and used report of company performance is the **Annual Report**. This document is written by company management and is designed to summarize the prior year's financial and business activities. Company management is encouraged, but not required, to provide forward-looking information as well. While there is some latitude in determining what is included in an Annual Report, a typical table of contents may look like this:

- Financial highlights
- Letter to shareholders
- Description of the company, its products, and its customers
- Management's discussion and analysis (MD&A)
- Statement of management's responsibility
- Independent Accountants opinion letter
- Financial Statements
    - Balance Sheet
    - Income Statement
    - Cash Flow Statement
    - Notes to the Financial Statements
- List of Officers and Board members
- Key company contacts

We will focus on the financial statements section of the Annual Report, as we interpret what information each of the components is designed to provide.

The **Balance Sheet** tells what the company owns and what the company owes, at a particular point in time. The difference is the "net worth" of the company. This is a "snapshot" of the company's financial position.

The **Income Statement** tells what the company's revenues and expenses were for the preceding period, typically a year. This is an historical view of what the company's operations accomplished.

The **Cash Flow Statement** tells what the company's primary sources and uses of cash were for the preceding period, typically a year.

The Notes to the Financial Statements explain in detail what is included in the aforementioned statements.

The **MD&A** (**management's discussion and analysis**) is usually in the first half of the annual report. Its purpose is to explain why the financial numbers are different from one period to the next.

Data Reliability

The financial information presented by a company is only valuable if it's relevant, reliable, timely, and consistent. Independent accountants (the

predicted\ value
verify
neutral
faithfulness

"auditors") attest to the fairness of the information in their "audit opinion" letter. They ensure that GAAP has been consistently applied.

GAAP can be overwhelming, in terms of numbers of rules and their complexity. But the principles tend to fall into 13 broad categories. See Exhibit 5.1.

There are times when two different techniques may be allowed to account for a transaction or report information. This intricacy will be covered in your accounting courses.

Supplemental Readings

- Company Annual Report
- *Balance Sheet Barrier* (video)

Summary

Companies whose shares are traded in the market must regularly comply with the obligation to supply financial information to investors and to the government. The Annual Report is the most popular financial report. With its financial statements, it shows a snapshot of the company's financial position, a summary of its operations, and sources and uses of cash.

Accounting characteristics

A. Relevance
    1. Predict
    2. ~~[illegible]~~ Timely
B. Reliable
    1. verifiable
    2. Rep. faithfulness
    3. Neutral
C. Comparability
D. Consistency
    every year the same
E. materiality
F. Conservatism

Chapter 5
Key Vocab Words

Exhibit 5.1: Fundamental Principles of Accounting

Entity: accounting records are separate from the owners

Going concern: we assume the company will continue to exist

Stable monetary unit: we assume no currency devaluation

Accountability: management serves at the discretion of the shareholders

Relevance: all relevant transactions are included
~ all idems that effect users judgement

Limited time periods: accounting reports must have a cut-off

Consistency: rules must be consistently applied
~ every year the same unless otherwise stated

Conservatism: estimates should err on the side of conservatism, present worst case senerio allowing for things to happen

Matching: all costs incurred in generating a period's revenues must be included in that period's operating results

Objectivity: financial data should have no bias

Disclosure: any and all important data should be reported

Free enterprise: we assume we operate in a capitalistic society

Substance over form: intent supersedes

materiality : under normal circumstances you would not search for a lost dime

Key Terms

Balance Sheet
Cash Flow Statement
Generally accepted accounting principles (GAAP)
Income Statement
Management's discussion and analysis (MD&A)
Proxy Statement
Securities and Exchange Commission (SEC)
SEC Forms:
- Form 8-K
- Form 10-K
- Form 10-Q

Name	**Date**	**Section**

Problems/Cases

P5-1 Obtain a corporate annual report and identify the following:

Company name ______________________

Assets' value ______________________

Net income ______________________

Sales or revenue value ______________________

Cash balance ______________________

Year-end/Cut-off date ______________________

Materials for Further Reference

Weygandt, Keiso, and Kell. *Accounting Principles*, 5th edition. New York: John Wiley & Sons, Inc., 1999.

Merrill Lynch. *How to Read a Financial Report.* New York, 1997.

Internet Web Sites to Explore

www.sec.gov

www.hoovers.com

www.wsrn.com/home/index.html

www.tsrn.com/wsc/corporate_snapshot.html

www.bloomberg.com

www.gov.sec

www.excite.elogic.com/sec

www.disclosure.com

www.edgar.sec.gov

PART FOUR

FINANCIAL INFORMATION - INTERPRETATION

In Part Four: Financial Information - Interpretation, Chapters 6-12 discuss specific aspects of financial information, to aid the reader in interpreting financial information. These chapters provide an introduction, skeletal outline, summary, and study aids for each of the major sections in *The Wall Street Journal Guide to Understanding Money and Investing.*

The key topics include the following:

Money (Chapter 6): history, forms, etc.
Stocks (Chapter 7): history, trading, risks, etc.
Bonds (Chapter 8): trading, risks, etc.
Mutual Funds (Chapter 9): trading, risks, etc.
Currencies (Chapter 11): examples, risks, etc.
Derivatives (Chapter 12): purposes, examples, risks, etc.

Chapter 10 explains the purposes of Investment Indexes as well as how to select and interpret the appropriate one to use as a benchmark.

Chapter 6

Money

Chapter Concepts

After mastering the material in this chapter, the reader will be able to:

- explain the importance of money as a store of value
- describe the money cycle in the United States
- identify various forms of money
- identify the roles of the Federal Reserve
- define money supply and each of its aggregate measures
- explain how money is used to measure economic health
- describe the economic cycle
- interpret money statistics presented in *The Wall Street Journal*

Background

Money is a store of value. When a transaction takes place, often the common denominator determining the "value" exchanged is quoted in terms of money. While exchanges in early civilization often involved only fungible goods ("**barter**"), exchanges have evolved to recognize exchange by "fiat" **currency**: money that has no intrinsic value, versus gold or silver coins, for example. Section I of *The Wall Street Journal Guide to Understanding Money and Investing* discusses "Money": its history, its various forms, its flows, and its value as an economic indicator. The role of the Federal Reserve is also discussed.

Supplemental Reading

- *The Wall Street Journal Guide to Understanding Money and Investing* (1993): "Money" pp. 4 - 27

Section Outline: WSJ Guide - Money

History

Paper Money

US Dollar

Money Cycle

Other Forms of Money

Federal Reserve System

Controlling the Money Flow

The Money Supply

Measuring Economic Health

Consumer Confidence

Consumer Price Index

Economic Cycle

The Federal Reserve

Established by the Federal Reserve Act of 1913, the Federal Reserve is chiefly responsible for regulating the nation's monetary policy. Its mission is to help keep employment levels high, inflation benign, and economic conditions sound. It also seeks to help prevent cyclical developments from having a negative effect on the economy.

One of the Fed's main tools in pursuing its primary objective is its policy regarding short-term interest rates. Typically, the Fed lowers rates (i.e. eases monetary policy) when it wants to stimulate economic activity and lessen the threat of economic recession. Conversely, the Fed has usually raised short-term interest rates (i.e. tightened monetary policy) when it wanted to slow the pace of growth to prevent a marked increase in inflation.

Changes in the US Currency

The wholesale revamping of US currency began in 1996 with the introduction of the new $100 bill. Its key features include:

- A larger offset portrait
- Concentric fine lines printed behind both the portrait and the building on the back
- A polymeric thread embedded vertically in the bill
- A watermark identical to the portrait visible from each side
- A number in the lower right corner which changes color (green/black) depending on the viewing angle.

Since 1996, the $50, $20, and $10 bills have also been modified. No changes to the $5 and $1 bills are planed since counterfeiting of these bills is uncommon.

Summary

Money is a store of value, allowing governments, households, and businesses to efficiently transact acquisitions and sales of goods and services. There is little, if any, contention regarding the value of money; even exchanging one currency for another (covered in more depth in Chapter 11) rarely involves disputes over the value of legal tender. With the general agreement that a currency represents value, economic measurements using that currency are rendered more reliable.

Key Terms

barter
Chairman of the Federal Reserve
consumer price index (CPI)
currency
economic cycle
federal reserve
inflation
leading economic indicators
M1
M2
M3
money
money cycle
money supply

Name Date Section

Review Questions

Q6-1 Identify the countries that use the term "dollar" for their currency.

Q6-2 Identify nicknames for the United States dollar.

Q6-3 Under what circumstances can the United States dollar be reproduced?

Q6-4 What recent changes have been made to US currency?

Q6-5 Identify each of the roles of the Federal Reserve.

Q6-6 Explain how the Federal Reserve "creates" money.

Q6-7 Identify the key leading economic indicators.

Q6-8 Describe what is meant by the economic cycle.

Name ______________________ Date ____________ Section ______

Exercises

E6-1 For each United States' monetary unit denomination, indicate whose picture is on the front, and what the key picture is on the back.

Name ____________________ **Date** __________ **Section** ______

E6-2 Identify the currency for each of the following countries:

United States ________________

Great Britain ________________

France ________________

Germany ________________

Switzerland ________________

Spain ________________

Japan ________________

China ________________

Russia ________________

Malaysia ________________

Mexico ________________

Name **Date** **Section**

E6-3 Identify the different "forms" of money.

E6-4 Differentiate among M1, M2, and M3.

Name Date Section

Problems/Cases

P6-1 Identify problems with the consumer price index and how these problems are being addressed.

Materials for Further Reference

Miller and Van Hoose. *Modern Money and Banking*, 3rd edition. New York: McGraw Hill, 1993.

Internet Web Sites to Explore

www.publicdebt.treas.gov/of/ofntebnd.htm

Chapter 7

Stocks

Chapter Concepts

After mastering the material in this chapter, the reader will be able to:

- describe what stock is
- differentiate between stocks and shares
- describe the advantages and disadvantages of stock ownership
- identify the key parties in a stock transaction
- describe the process of stock selection, ownership, and sale
- identify various markets where stocks are traded
- interpret stock data presented in *The Wall Street Journal*

Background

As described in Chapter 4, there are three basic forms of business organization: sole proprietorship, partnership, and corporation. Stock represents ownership in a corporation. When an investor buys stock s/he becomes an owner of the company, called a **stockholder**, **shareholder**, or stock owner.

The investor's percentage ownership depends on three factors:
1. how many shares s/he owns;
2. how many shares the corporation has issued and "authorized";
3. how many shares of these "authorized" shares are held by investors ("outstanding shares").

For example, if an investor owns 1,000 shares of stock in a corporation that has 1,000,000 shares authorized, issued and outstanding, the investor has a .1% (1,000/1,000,000) ownership stake. As you will see in "Stocks" (Section II in *The Wall Street Guide to Understanding Money and Investing*), stocks are a fascinating feature of a capitalistic society. The wealth potential (and risk potential!) of stock ownership and all the industries that serve such a process have been the source of much fame, fortune, and failure.

Supplemental Readings

- *The Wall Street Journal Guide to Understanding Money and Investing* (1993): "Stocks" pp. 34 - 81
- Appendix B

ASSETS = LIABILITIES + OWNERS EQUITY

STOCK HOLDER - SHARE HOLDER

-OWNER OF A CORP.

COMMON STOCKS - TRADED, PUBLICALLY OWNED

~~PREFE~~ PFD STOCK - DO NOT OWN THE COMPANY

XYZ PFD (1.80 dividend) - BUYING DIVIDEND INCOME - PAY FIRST

XYZ (1.00) - NO GUARANTEE

NO DIVIDEND CAN BE PAID UNTIL PREFERED STOCK DIVIDEND IS PAID

SPLIT STOCK

XYZ - $100 PER SHARE

1,000,000 SHARES OUT STANDING

MARKET VALUE = 100,000,000

2 FOR 1 STOCK SPLIT

2,000,000 SHARES OUTSTANDING

MARKET VALUE = 100,000,000

$50 PER SHARE

REVERSE SPLIT - EXTREMELY BAD

VOTING - ELECT DIRECTORS

PROXY STATEMENT

BALLET - PROXY TO VOTE FOR DIRECTORS

VALUE OF A STOCK

RETURN ON INVESTMENT - MONEY WIN OR LOSS ON STOCK

XYZ = $50

$5,000 => 100 SHARES

INVESTMENT

$6,000 +20% INCREASE (INCREASE IN VALUE OF STOCK (CAPITAL GAIN)

RETURN ON INVESTMENT = $1000

Section Outline: WSJ Guide - Stocks

Stocks: Sharing a Corporation

The Right to Vote

The Value of Stock

The Stock Certificate

Selling New Stock

Stock Buyers

Buying Stocks

Selling Short

Buying on Margin

Stock Quotations

Reading the Stock Tables

Sifting Stock Information

Evaluating Companies

The Traditional Stock Market

SELLING NEW STOCK

Trading on the NYSE

I.P.O. - INITIAL PUBLIC OFFERING (1ST TIME)
- SECONARY OFFERING

The Electronic Stock Market

INDIVIDUAL INVESTORS
INSTITUTIONAL - INVESTING OTHER PEOPLES MONEY
BUY LARGE AMOUNTS
BIG INVESTORS IN A COMPANY

Reading the Averages

Market Indexes

STOCK PRICE x STOCKS OUTSTAND

Market Cycles

MARKET CAPITALIZATION
5 BILLION - LARGE CAP
1.5 - 5 BILL - MIDDLE CAP
↓ 1.5 BILL - SMALL CAP

Crash

Traders Around the Clock

DIVIDEND YEILD
A (1.00) $25/SHARE
YEILD - ~~25%~~ ~~40%~~ 4%

Tracking International Markets

B (1.00) $50/SHARE
YEILD - 2%

The World Stock Index

~~STREET NAME & TRADE~~
CUSIP NUMBER - EVERY COMPANY GETS ONE OF THESE NUMBERS

International Investing

INCOME STOCK - PAYS A HIGH DIVIDEND
GROSS STOCK - LOOKING 4 GROWTH VS. HIGH DIVIDEND
DIVIDEND YEILD - WHAT YOU PUT IN VS. WHAT YOU GET OUT

DIVIDEND (~~PROFIT~~) / PRICE = YEILD

PAR VALUE - WORTHLESS NUMBER
MEANING LESS FOR STOCKS

Summary

Owning stock means owning a part of a corporation, even if it is only a tiny percentage. Stock ownership carries with it potential advantages such as price appreciation, dividends, and corporate voting power. But there are disadvantages as well, including price fluctuations and/or substantial price declines. But as discussed in Chapter 4, the maximum loss is the value of your investment.

The actual process of purchasing and selling stocks is really quite simple. But searching for, analyzing, and selecting stocks can be a difficult and time consuming process. With over 700,000,000 shares traded on a typical day on the New York Stock Exchange alone, there are lots of buyers and sellers, each looking to buy a bargain and/or dump a loser. The price for any stock transaction is that price which the willing buyer and the willing seller agree to, each party presumably satisfied with the "deal".

The Wall Street Journal, as is true of other business periodicals, presents the results of such transactions each day, giving the best evidence of the value of each share of stock: the price at which a willing buyer bought and a willing seller sold.

Significant interpretation and analysis of a corporation's activities are needed to make an informed purchase or sale decision. Chapter 5 introduced the interpretation of financial reporting, a logical, initial step in stock analysis.

BUYING STOCK

CALL BROKERAGE HOUSE
DEALER ACTUALLY DOES THE TRADE

DEALER QUOTE 25 1/4 - 3/8 — GUARENTEE 100 SHARES
ROUND LOT ✓
ODD LOT - 50 SHARES
WILL BUY FOR MORE AND SELL FOR LESS

SELLING SHORT - DON'T DO IT
BUY ON MARGIN ✓
- LOSE A LOT OF MONEY QUICKLY
SELLING STOCK YOU DO NOT OWN
BORROW STOCK FROM ANOTHER ACCOUNT
WHEN SELL SHORT ITS BORROWED STOCKS AND YOU WANT STOCK TO GO DOWN

MARGIN
BORROW MONEY TO PAY FOR STOCK
YOU WANT STOCK TO GO UP
LEAVERAGE - BUYING STOCK ON BORROWED MONEY

EASIEST WAY TO GET STOCK INFO IS THE INTERNET
NEVER GET STOCK INFO FROM CHAT ROOMS

EVALUATING A STOCK
EARNINGS PER SHARE = EPS
TOTAL EARNINGS ÷ # OF SHARES

$\frac{\text{OWNERS EQUITY}}{\text{NUMBER OF SHARES}}$ = BOOK VALUE (EQUITY)

COMPARE STOCK PRICE TO BOOK VALUE

DIVIDEND PER SHARE
PAY OUT RATIO - MEASURE OF WHAT PAID OUT

$\frac{\text{DIV}}{\text{EPS}}$ = PAYOUT RATIO — EPS = 5.00, DIV = 1.00 = 20%

RETURN ON EQUITY
BOOK VALUE = $50.00 A SHARE
RETURN ON EQUITY = $\frac{5}{50}$ = 10% $\frac{\text{EPS}}{\text{BOOK VALUE}}$

Chapter 8

Bonds

Chapter Concepts

After mastering the material in this chapter, the reader will be able to:

- describe what a bond is
- identify the key parties in a bond transaction
- identify the advantages and disadvantages of bond ownership
- describe the process of bond selection, ownership and sale/redemption
- interpret bond data presented in *The Wall Street Journal*

Background

While stocks represent "ownership", bonds represent "loanership". Instead of owning a piece of a corporation, like an investor does when s/he owns shares of stock, a bond investor has made a loan to a corporation (or governmental unit). The bondholder (the investor) loans money to the corporation or governmental unit (the borrower). The bondholder expects two things in return for the loan:
1. interest (usually annually or semiannually)
2. principal repayment (at the end of the loan period).

For example, if you buy a 10-year AT&T bond for $1,000 that pays 9% interest, you expect two things in return:
1. interest each year for 10 years ($1,000 x .09 = $90)
2. principal at the end of the 10-year period ($1,000).

As with stocks, many bonds are actively traded. In other words, you may be able to sell your bond to another investor prior to its maturity. Several factors are involved in determining the value of a bond, including the borrower's financial position, the current interest rate situation, years to maturity, etc. Section III of *The Wall Street Journal Guide to Understanding Money and Investing and Investing* describes bonds in much detail.

Supplemental Readings

- *The Wall Street Journal Guide to Understanding Money and Investing* (1993): "Bonds" pp. 82 - 103
- Appendix B

Section Outline: WSJ Guide - Bonds

Bonds: Financing the Future

The Bond Certificate

Figuring a Bond's Worth

Rating Bonds

Tracking Bond Performance

Municipal Bonds

U.S. Treasury Bonds, Notes, Bills

A Bond Vocabulary

Buying and Trading Bonds

Other Bonds, Other Choices

The World of Bonds

Term Structure of Interest Rates

An investor who chooses to invest in bonds is typically interested in the interest income. A knowledgeable investor, before investing in a bond, needs financial information, including what the going rates of interest are in the economy. These going rates of interest are often graphically depicted in what is known as a **yield curve**. The yield curve is the graphical basis for depicting the **term structure of interest rates.**

Generally, the term structure of interest rates describes:
1. the relationship among short, intermediate and long-term interest rates
2. depicted by a yield curve
3. as of a point in time
4. using government securities.

The yield curve is developed by plotting on an XY chart the **yield-to-maturity** on government securities of various maturities.

See Exhibit 8.1.

Exhibit 8.1: Term Structure of Interest Rates

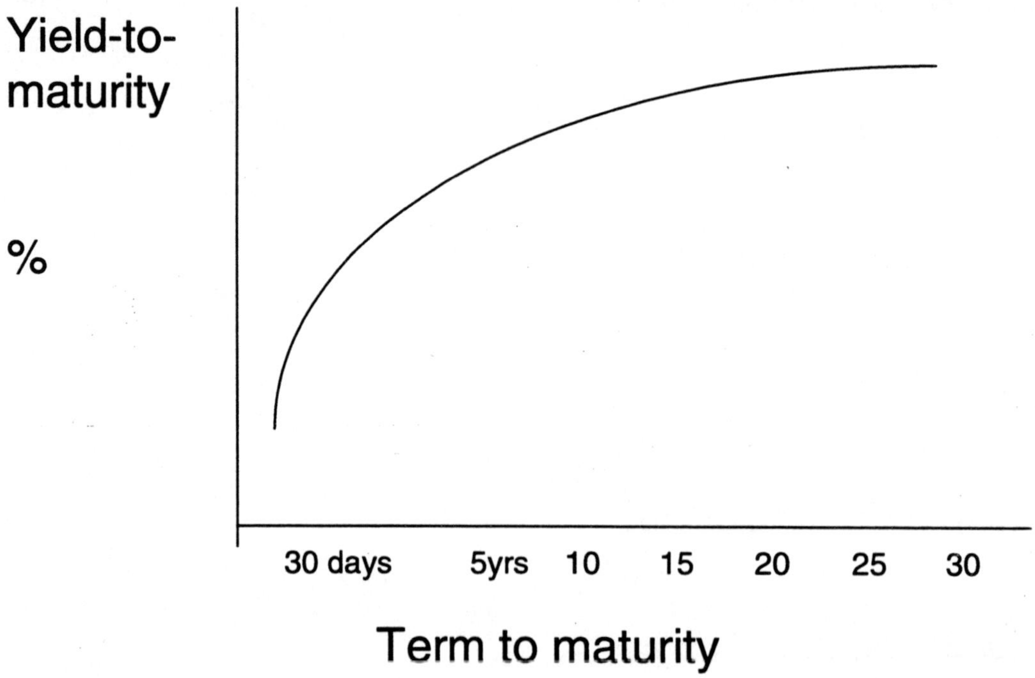

BONDS

OCT. 18

BOND - BORROWING

YOU ARE THE LENDER
LENDER IS THE ONE THEY ARE PAYING BACK

LENDER
- INTEREST
- WHO?
- PAY BACK
- WHEN ARE YOU GETTING PAID BACK

PAYBACK
└ AMOUNT LENT => PRINCIPAL (PAR VALUE)
INTEREST => INTEREST RATE -> COUPON RATE
WHO => BORROWER
WHEN => MATURITY DATE
(HOW LONG) => TERM
# of YRS

10,000	TJA CORP. (BORROWER)	12%	10/18/08

PAY 1/2 EVERY SIX MONTHS

> STRONG ON ACCOUNTING PRINCIPLES + OBJECTIVES
> CALCULTIONS FOR PROJECT WILL BE ON FINAL
> ANYTHING FROM FIRST TEST

IF YOU BUY ON INTERNET IT IS REGIESTERED ON STREET NAME

1,000	TJA	6%	10/18/08
1,000	TJA	9%	10/18/04
1,000	TJA	14.99%	10/18/09
1,000	TJA	30%	10/18/29

~~HIGER~~
HIGHER RISK
⬇
HIGHER RATE

↑
RISK OF ABILITY TO PAY BACK
LONGER THE MATURITY THE HIGHER RISK
RISKS - INFLATION AND BORROWER RISK

YIELD CURVE

NEGATIVE YIELD CURVE: LONG TIME LOWER INTEREST RATE: SO PEOPLE ONLY LEND GOVT MONEY FOR A SHORT TIME

1000 U.S. TREASURY 6.3 8/31/29
↑
ELIMINATE RISK

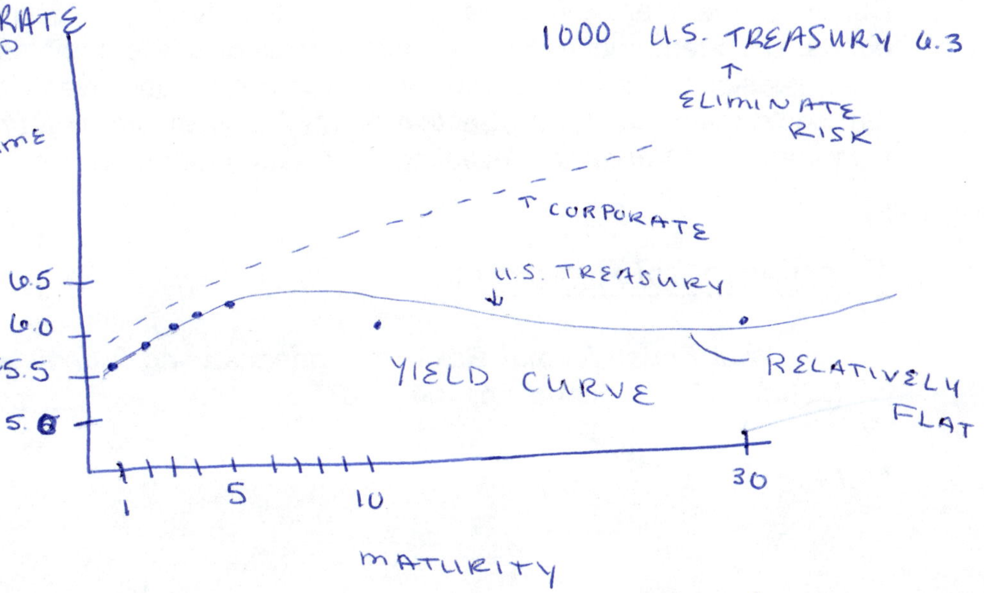

ALWAYS DRAW YIELD CURVE USING GOV'T BONDS B/C YOU ELIMINATE BORROWERS RISK

$1,000
STATED RATE 9%
MARKET RATE 10.%
} MAKE LESS ON THIS INVESTMENT

/ MAKE ON OTHER INVESTMENTS

Chapter 9

Mutual Funds

Chapter Concepts

After mastering the material in this chapter, the reader will be able to:

- describe what a mutual fund is
- identify key parties to a mutual fund transaction
- describe the advantages and disadvantages of mutual funds
- describe the process of mutual fund selection, purchase, ownership, and sale
- interpret mutual fund data presented in *The Wall Street Journal*

Background

The popularity of **mutual funds** exploded in the 1980s and 1990s. A mutual fund is an investment company usually organized by an advisory firm for the purpose of offering the fund's shareholders a specific investment objective.

Currently, there are more than 9,000 mutual funds, investing in stocks, bonds, short-term money market instruments, or some combination thereof. If an investor has an investment need, there may be several mutual funds that could meet that need. Section IV of *The Wall Street Journal Guide to Understanding Money and Investing* describes mutual funds in much detail.

Supplemental Readings

- *The Wall Street Journal Guide to Understanding Money and Investing* (1993): "Mutual Funds" pp. 104 - 123

- Appendix B

*MON IS 6-8 GRISWOLD LECTURE HALL

Section Outline: WSJ Guide - Mutual Funds

MUTUAL FUNDS

HOW MUCH RISK ARE YOU WILLING TO TAKE?

Mutual Funds: Putting It Together

The Mutual Fund Market

MULTIPLE FUNDS → FIDELITY, T. ROWE PRICE → COMPANY

Targeted Investments

EASIER TO TRADE WITHIN FAMILIES, HARD TO SWITCH FAMILY

Special Purpose Funds

BY LAW THEY ARE REQUIRED TO GIVE YOU A PROSPECTUS BEFORE BUY

Inside a Mutual Fund

→ PROSPECTUS - FULL DETAILS, HOW OBJECTIVES OF BONDS, HOW THEY ARE MANAGE & FEES, WHO MANAGE

Mutual Fund Quotations

It's All In the Charts

→ FEES - 1% A YEAR

Tracking Fund Performance

INDEX FUNDS

The Prospectus

International Funds

TWO WAYS TO MAKE MONEY
1. APPECIATION
2. DIVIDEND + INTEREST

ROUND LOT - 100 SHARES

PROFESSIONAL
- MANAGE YOUR MONEY
- HIRED

*MONEY IS THROWN INTO A POOL OF MONEY

*OBJECTIVES: WHAT THE PREFERENCE OF THE PERSON IS, HOW MUCH THEY ARE WILLING TO LOSE.

TYPES OF FUNDS (ALL COMPANIES)

I. STOCK FUNDS — MUCH MORE RISK
- GROWTH: NO DIVIDENDS, PUT MONEY BACK INTO COMPANY
- GROWTH & INCOME
  → DIVIDENDS ARE PAID
  → POSSIBILITY TO LOSS AND GAIN QUICKLY

II. BOND FUNDS
- TAXABLE — TREASURY (NO RISK), WHAT BONDS ARE THEY BUYING
- NON-TAXABLE — MUNICIPLE BONDS - SCHOOLS, CITIES, FEDERAL

FEDERAL TAXES

III. INDEX FUND
- DOW JONES INDUSTRIAL AVERAGE
  → LOWER FEES DUE TO NOT HAVING TO PAY FOR UPPER KNOWLEDGE
- S&P 500
  → FOLLOW INDEX BECAUSE THEY BUY ALL THE STOCKS IN THE INDEX OR THAT PART OF THE MARKET
- NASDAQ

IV. MONEY MARKEK MUTUAL FUND
- PARKING PLACE FOR MONEY
- EARN SOME INTEREST
- CAN WRITE CHECKS ON THEM
- HARD TO GET MONEY INTO THEM
- HARD TO WORK WITH
- WHEN BUY OR SELL STOCK THEY TAKE IT OUT RIGHT AWAY OR PUT IT IN

MUTUAL FUND: MONEY INVESTED BY A NUMBER OF INVESTORS AND INVESTED IN LARGE NUMBERS OF SECURITIES (STOCKS / BONDS)

BOUGHT 10 SHARES @ $10 1/15/XX
SOLD 10 SHARES @ $17 6/15/XX
→ TAXED ON THE $7 INCOME

ROTH IRA - RETIREMENT INCOME
2,000 MAX CONTRIBUTION IS TAXED, BUT NOT INCOME

Summary

Mutual funds are becoming the investment vehicle of choice for many investors. However, investors need to proceed cautiously. Mutual funds have several advantages and disadvantages.
Advantages include:

- professional management
- diversification
- low unit costs
- numerous choices
- clear investment objective

Disadvantages include:

- fees
- most do not beat market benchmarks
- impersonal nature of the investment
- taxes are outside the control of the investor

Key Terms

bond funds
closed end funds
closed funds
global funds
international funds
investment objectives
money market funds
mutual fund
mutual fund family
open end funds
open funds
prospectus
stock funds

Name Date Section

Review Questions

Q9-1 Identify the key types of mutual funds.

Q9-2 Discuss the advantages of mutual funds.

Q9-3 Discuss the disadvantages of mutual funds.

Name ______________________ Date ____________ Section ______

Exercises

E9-1 Select three mutual funds (each from a different mutual fund family) from *The Wall Street Journal* and record their quotations below.

Name	Date	Section

E9-2 For one of the mutual funds in E9-1, explain in your own words what is being reported.

Name **Date** **Section**

Problems/Cases

P9-1 Locate two bond funds and two stock funds in *The Wall Street Journal*. Research these funds via *Morningstar*. Compare performance to an appropriate benchmark. Interpret the information you have obtained for these funds.

Materials for Further Reference

Bogle, John. *Bogle on Mutual Funds*. New York: Irwin, 1994.

CDA/Wiesenberger Mutual Funds Report.

Directory of Mutual Funds. Investment Company Institute.

The Individual Investor's Guide to Low-Load Mutual Funds, 18th Edition. American Association of Individual Investors, 1999.

Morningstar Mutual Funds. Morningstar, Inc.

Mutual Fund Fact Book. Investment Company Institute.

Internet Web Sites to Explore

www.morningstar.net

www.smartmoney.com

www.thomsoninvest.net

www.mfea.com

www.scudder.com

www.vanguard.com

www.fundalarm.com

www.investormap.com

www.lipperweb.com

www.findafund.com

www.paulmerriman.com

www.personalwealth.com

www.wallstreetcity.com

www.fidelity.com

www.strong-funds.com

www.troweprice.com

www.fundspot.com

www.fundsinteractive.com

www.mfcafe.com

Chapter 10

Investment Indexes

Chapter Concepts

After mastering the material in this chapter, the reader will be able to:

- explain the purpose of indexes in evaluating investment performance
- identify key investment indexes used for stocks and bonds
- differentiate among different stock indexes
- choose the right index to use as a benchmark
- calculate a stock market index using two different methods
- interpret investment indexes presented in *The Wall Street Journal*

Background

"Performance is relative": LJM.

Numbers alone do not usually tell a full story; they must be compared to something else. A person is usually considered a failure if s/he fails 7 times out of 10. Yet if that person is a baseball player, that record yields a .300 batting average, usually good enough to make it to Cooperstown!!

If you say Northwood University won 10 games, is that good or bad? Does it not depend upon the time period and the sport? Winning 10 games in one season is quite an accomplishment for the football team, yet a poor showing for basketball, especially if we count both the men's and women's teams!! All performance must be evaluated against appropriate **benchmarks**. Investment performance is no exception.

Is a 10% Return on Your Investments Good?

You have just received notice of the performance returns of the trust your Great Aunt Lucille set up for you. The investments provided a return of 10.0%!! Are you happy or sad? Is 10% a good rate of return? Perhaps you need to ask some questions... Perhaps you need some financial information!

- Over what time period(s) were the returns earned?
- How much risk was taken?
- What investments were in the trust?
- What percentage of the trust is represented by each investment?
- What was the performance of each individual investment?
- What returns were earned on comparable investments?

Answers to these questions begin to give you a clearer picture of whether a 10% return was good or bad.

Investment Indexes

An **index** is a standard against which financial performance can be compared. Indexes or "benchmarks" exist for nearly every type of investment. Most are updated and reported on a regular basis; some continuously throughout the business day. The primary categories of investment indexes are stock indexes and bond indexes. Indexes for other types of investments are also popular, including indexes for money market funds, mutual funds, real estate, collectibles, currencies, commodities, etc. We will concentrate on stock indexes and bond indexes. See Exhibit 10.1 for a description of the key attributes of a good index.

Exhibit 10.1: Hallmarks of a Good Investment Index

A good investment index should:

1. be easily replicated
2. be accepted as a good surrogate
3. have a long history of reliable data
4. have ongoing data reported regularly

Stock Indexes

Stock indexes fall into two broad categories: US stock indexes and non-US indexes. The US stock indexes we will focus on are the Dow Jones Industrial Average (DJIA), the Standard & Poor's 500, the NYSE Composite, the NASDAQ, the Wilshire 5000, the Russell 2000, the AMEX, and Value Line.

Exhibit 10.2 shows a summary of these US stock market indexes as well as two other non-US stock indexes. As you can see, key distinguishing features among the indexes are the following: focus; number of securities; calculation method; and current value. Each of these indexes focuses on a different subset of the stock market. For example, the S&P 500 (Standard & Poor's 500) focuses on a cross-section of 500 of the largest firms in the USA, while the Russell 2000 focuses on 2,000 of the smaller firms in the USA. This exhibit also indicates the number of securities in each index. Often, as you can see, the number of securities is right in the name of the index!

Three basic methods can be used to calculate an index: simple arithmetic average; value-weighted average; and geometric average. The **simple average**, used by the DJIA, is calculated by adding the price per share of each of the 30 companies in the DJIA and dividing by a special factor: the divisor. Originally, when the DJIA expanded to 30 companies in 1928, this factor was 30. But due to replacements in the companies in the DJIA, stock splits, and other changes, that factor has changed. The factor is quoted in *The Wall Street Journal* each day. In a later section in this chapter, we will further explore the DJIA.

Although calculating a simple average is indeed "simple", it is wrought with potential problems. For example, should a $1 change in a $150 stock have the same impact on the index as a $1 change in a $15 stock? It does with a simple average!

The **value-weighted average**, used by most indexes, eliminates the problem just highlighted in the simple average. The value-weighted average takes into account the total equity value of each company in the index, not just the value of one share of its stock. The value-weighted average is computed by multiplying the number of shares outstanding of each company by its market price and then summing each of these calculations before dividing by a factor to arrive at the index. Using this method ensures that changes in stock prices are weighted according to the total equity value of the respective company.

Geometric averages are quite rare; Value Line is the only major index to use such a method. This complicated mathematical method attempts to refine the impact of individual stock price changes on the value of the index overall.

Two other commonly used indexes used to measure stock market activity are the MS-EAFE and the DJWSI. The MS-EAFE (Morgan Stanley - Europe, Australia, and Far East) is a value-weighted index that measures the stock performance of a representative number of stocks outside the USA. This index would be useful in evaluating the performance of a portfolio of stocks outside the USA. The DJWSI (Dow Jones World Stock Index) is a value weighted average of stocks around the globe, including both USA and non-USA stocks. The MS-EAFE and DJWSI are also included in Exhibit 10.2.

Exhibit 10.2: Key Stock Market Indexes: USA, International, & Global

Index	*Focus*	*Number of Companies*	*6/99* Value*
Dow Jones Industrial Average	established firms	30	10,971
S&P 500	largest US firms	500	1,373
NYSE Composite	NYSE firms	3,046	648
NASDAQ	Hi-Tech firms	5,487	2,686
AMEX	financials, natural resources	771	798
Value Line	cross-section	1,700	466
Russell 2000	small firms	2,000	458
Wilshire 5000	all NYSE, AMEX, plus large NASDAQ firms	5,000	12,584
DJWSI	firms around the world	Varies	157
MS-EAFE	large int'l firms	Varies	1,451

*Source: *The Wall Street Journal*, July 1, 1999

Generally speaking, each major stock exchange has its own stock index. Exhibit 10.3 shows several major countries and their stock market index.

Exhibit 10.3: Non-USA Markets/Exchanges

Country	Exchange/Index	6/99 Value*
Canada	**Toronto 300 Composite**	**7,010**
Mexico	**Bolsa**	**5,830**
Brazil	**Bovespa**	**11,627**
United Kingdom	**London Financial Times 100 share**	**6,319**
Germany	**Frankfurt XETRA-DAX**	**5,379**
France	**Paris CAC 40**	**4,537**
Japan	**Tokyo Nikkei 225 Average**	**17,530**
Hong Kong	**Hang Seng**	**13,532**
Singapore	**Straits Times**	**2,168**
Australia	**All Ordinaries Index**	**2,969**

* Source: *The Wall Street Journal*, July 1, 1999

Bond Indexes

The number of bond indexes is much more limited than the number of stock indexes. The most popular is the Lehman Brothers T-Bond index, quoted daily in *The Wall Street Journal*. This benchmark represents a composite index of Treasury securities' yield and price performance.

Other bond indexes widely quoted include:

DJ 20 Bond - provides the average price and yield of 10 public utility bonds and 10 industrial bonds.

Salomon Mortgage-Backed - covers mortgage-backed securities such as Ginnie Maes, Fannie Maes, and Freddie Macs.

Bond Buyer Municipal - covers AA-rated and A-rated municipal bonds.

Merrill Lynch Corporate - a corporate bond composite.

Create Your Own Index!

Let's say you have exactly half your investments in small capitalization stocks and exactly half in French stocks. How do you judge your portfolio's performance? Why not construct your own index!! You could take 50% of the Russell 2000 index performance for the period and 50% of the CAC index for the same period and add them together. Voila! You have an index tailored to your portfolio!

Dow Jones Industrial Average

When your hear: "the market was up today", most likely you have just found out that the **Dow Jones Industrial Average** (DJIA) increased. Most people, when referring to "the market", are really talking about the DJIA. Even though the DJIA has only 30 stocks in it (yet there are more than 30,000 corporations in the USA), and the index is calculated as a simple average (a $1 increase in a $15 stock is offset by a $1 decrease in a $150 stock), we are creatures of habit. The DJIA is the most recognized, quoted, and used stock market average in the world. Part of its attraction is the fact that it has been around for over 100 years, having celebrated its centennial on May 26, 1996.

Why only 30 companies and why a simple average? Consider that when originally devised, there was no such thing as a computer or calculator! All these calculations had to be done by hand! Also consider that the USA was evolving from an agricultural economy to an industrial economy and corporations were no where near as numerous as they are today. Note that originally there were only 11 companies in the average. This number was soon increased to 12, then increased to 20 in 1916 and to 30 in 1928. Charles H. Dow, who developed the industrial average while he was the original editor of *The Wall Street Journal*, produced his first market average in 1884. The first industrial average followed two years later.

From time to time, changes are made in the composition of the DJIA: a company is removed and replaced with another. The purpose of such changes is to make the index as representative as possible of the US stock market. In 1997, multiple changes to the DJIA were made. Additions and deletions at that time were as follows:

Addition	*Deletion*
Travelers Group	Westinghouse Electric
Hewlett Packard	Texaco
Johnson & Johnson	Bethlehem Steel
Wal-Mart Stores	Woolworth

"The changes", according to *The Wall Street Journal*, "will enlarge representation of the technology, finance, and health-care sectors." This change was the biggest change in the DJIA since June 1959, when four other companies were replaced. Sometimes changes are necessitated by a DJIA-company being acquired by or merged with another company, as occurred in 1998 when Citicorp and Travelers Group combined to form Citigroup. As you can see, Travelers Group, as a stand-alone company, didn't last long in the Dow Jones Industrial Average! The original 30 stocks in the DJIA and their 1999 counterparts are presented in Exhibit 10.4.

As you can see in Exhibit 10.4, there are only four carry-overs from the "original 30". Also, notice the number of changes just within the last 15 years: 18 positions have changed!

Exhibit 10.4: Stocks Used to Calculate the DJIA - Dow Jones Industrial Average

As of October 1, 1928	*As of June 30, 1999**
Allied Chemical & Die	**Allied-Chemical ('85)**
North American	**American Express ('82)**
Victor Talking Machine	**AT&T ('39)**
International Nickel	**Boeing ('87)**
International Harvester	**Caterpillar ('91)**
Goodrich	**Chevron ('84)**
Texas Gulf Sulphur	**Citigroup ('98)**
U.S. Steel	**Coca-Cola ('87)**
American Sugar	**Walt Disney ('91)**
American Tobacco	**DuPont ('35)**
Standard Oil (NJ)	**Eastman Kodak ('30)**
General Electric	**Exxon ('72)**
General Motors	**General Electric**
Atlantic Refining	**General Motors**
Texas Corporation	**Goodyear ('30)**
Chrysler	**Hewlett Packard ('97)**
Paramount Publix	**IBM ('32-'39;'79)**
Bethlehem Steel	**International Paper ('56)**
General Railway Signal	**Johnson & Johnson ('97)**
Mack Trucks	**McDonald's ('85)**
American Smelting	**Merck ('79)**
American Can	**3M ('76)**
Postum Inc.	**J. P. Morgan ('91)**
Nash Motors	**Philip Morris ('85)**
Sears Roebuck	**Proctor & Gamble ('32)**
Westinghouse Electric	**Sears Roebuck**
Union Carbide	**Union Carbide**
Radio Corporation	**United Technologies ('75)**
Woolworth	**Wal-Mart Stores ('97)**

* The year the stock was added to the index is identified in parenthesis for those stocks that were not part of the original group.

Supplemental Reading

- *The Wall Street Journal Guide to Understanding Money and Investing* (1993): "Stocks" pp. 66 - 69; 76 - 79

Key Terms

benchmarking
Dow Jones Industrial Average
geometric average
index
NASDAQ
simple average
Standard & Poors
Value Line
value-weighted average

Name Date Section

Review Questions

Q10-1 Identify the key investment indexes for stocks and bonds.

Q10-2 Identify the key investment indexes for bonds.

Q10-3 Identify the four key attributes of a good investment index.

Q10-4 Identify the disadvantages of using the DJIA as a market index.

______________________________ ____________ ______

Name **Date** **Section**

Exercises

E10-1 For each type of investment below, indicate the best investment index to use as a benchmark:

IBM common stock ______________

Microsoft common stock ______________

Foreign stock ______________

Small cap stock ______________

Corporate bond ______________

Name	Date	Section

Problems/Cases

P10-1 Compute the Dow Jones Industrial Average for a specific date using *The Wall Street Journal* for the 30 stock prices and the "divisor". Why might your answer be different than the quoted market index? If you calculated the index using a value-weighted index approach how would your answer be different?

DJIA Stock	**Symbol**	**Price**
Allied-Chemical	________	________
American Express	________	________
AT&T	________	________
Boeing	________	________
Caterpillar	________	________
Chevron	________	________
Citigroup	________	________
Coca-Cola	________	________
Walt Disney	________	________
DuPont	________	________
Eastman Kodak	________	________
Exxon	________	________
General Electric	________	________
General Motors	________	________
Goodyear	________	________
Hewlett Packard	________	________
IBM	________	________
International Paper	________	________
Johnson & Johnson	________	________
McDonald's	________	________
Merck	________	________
3M	________	________
J. P. Morgan	________	________
Philip Morris	________	________
Proctor & Gamble	________	________
Sears Roebuck	________	________
Union Carbide	________	________
United Technologies	________	________
Wal-Mart Stores	________	________

Materials for Further Reference

Amling and Droms. *Investment Fundamentals.* Ft. Worth, TX: 1994.

Ibbottson Associates. *Stocks, bonds, Bills, and Inflation Yearbook.*

Internet Web Sites to Explore

www.prophetcharts.com

Chapter 11

Currencies

Chapter Concepts

After mastering the material in this chapter, the reader will be able to:

- appreciate the significance of fluctuating exchange rates
- understand the difference between currency appreciation and depreciation
- convert any amount of one currency into the corresponding amount of any other currency
- price goods and services in any currency
- interpret currency data presented in *The Wall Street Journal*

Background

The changing values of different currencies affect everyone, even if you never leave your native country. How? Many of the goods you buy either have components that were made in another country or the product itself could have a competitive threat from an imported product.

We live in a global economy, where the goods purchased may have originated from one of several different countries. We will look at changing exchange rates and their effect on consumers.

Exchange Rates

Assume you have been working hard to save enough money for the car of your dreams: a Jaguar XK8 convertible! The dealer quotes you a price of $60,000 for the car, which is to be imported from England.

The dealer suggests you consider a European Delivery Plan, whereby you fly to the United Kingdom to tour the Jaguar factory, pick up your car, test out your dream machine, and then have the car shipped back to the USA.

This plan would cost £ 38,000, including flights, hotels, and all other expenses. Note: £ stands for pounds sterling, the currency unit in the United Kingdom. Should you take delivery here in the USA or in England? What financial information would you like to have? You need to know the **exchange rate**! This is this rate at which you can buy pounds sterling for US dollars.

Looking at the "Key Currency Cross Rates" in *The Wall Street Journal* (Section C, you note that the exchange rate is 0.67728 by looking down the "dollar" column until you reach the "UK" row. (See p.28 in *The Wall Street Journal Guide to Understanding Money and Investing*). What does this number mean? The exchange rate reads as follows: 0.67728£/$. "For every $1, you can buy 0.67728 pounds sterling."

If you accept the European Delivery Plan, you will need to pay for the car in pounds sterling. How do you do that? Go to a major bank and buy £!! How many dollars will you need to buy £ 38,000? How many pounds sterling would the $60,000 price tag buy? Review the following two calculations:

1. $ 60,000 x 0.67728 £/$ = £ 40,637
2. £ 38,000 / 0.67728 £/$ = $ 56,107

These calculations tell you the following:

1. Your $60,000 purchase opportunity is equivalent to spending £ 40,637.
2. The European Delivery Plan of £ 40,000 is equivalent to a purchase price of $56,107, a savings of $3,893!! ($60,000 - $56,107). This represents savings of 6.5%!

But what if the exchange rate changes before you make up your mind? You have been following the £ for the last month, noting that it has gone from 0.7000 £/$ to 0.67728 £/$. What does this mean and what are the implications for your impending purchase?

The £ has appreciated and the US dollar has depreciated (although not by the same percentage). A month ago, $1 would buy 0.7000 £. Now $1 will buy only 0.67728 £, about 0.3 £ fewer! The pound sterling is getting more expensive ... and so is your car! However, as long as the exchange rate stays above 0.6333 £/$, (£ 38,000 / $60,000), the European Delivery Plan is cheaper.

When comparing one currency to another, if the exchange rate changes (and they often do ... daily or even more often!), one currency will have appreciated while the other depreciated. How do you tell which currency has appreciated and which currency has depreciated? Hint: focus on the exchange rate conversion. In our example, (£ and $US), the exchange rate was quoted in European terms: £/$. Most US exchange rates are quoted in European terms: foreign currency / $US. An exception is the United Kingdom Pound Sterling, which is most often quoted in **American terms**: $US / Pound Sterling. A quotation expressed as a foreign currency unit per US dollar is referred to as **European terms**, while a quotation expressed as dollars per unit of foreign currency is expressed as American or US Equivalent terms.

Focus on the denominator when trying to determine which currency is **appreciating** and which is **depreciating**. If the exchange rate quantity goes ***up*** in an exchange rate expressed in European terms, i.e. foreign currency / $US, the denominator currency (i.e. the US dollar) is appreciating, and the numerator currency is depreciating. If the exchange rate goes ***down***, the denominator currency is depreciating and the numerator currency is appreciating.

The Euro

Effective January 1,1999, electronic commerce in key European countries was transacted in a new currency: the Euro. The 11 countries participating in the agreement were: Austria, Belgium, Finland, France, Germany, Ireland, Italy, Luxembourg, The Netherlands, Portugal, and Spain. Notably absent are Denmark, Sweden, and the United Kingdom, which have chosen not to join this part of the "European Monetary Union" at this time.

Currency transaction in Euro will commence with bank notes and coins issued January 1, 2002 with June 30, 2002 as the final date for use of the sovereign currencies of these 11 participating countries. Will this attempt at a pan-European currency be successful? Only time will tell.

Supplemental Reading

- *The Wall Street Journal Guide to Understanding Money and Investing* (1993): "Money" pp. 28 – 33.

Section Outline: WSJ Guide - Money

The World of Money

Trading Money

Money Away From Home

Summary

International finance, of which we have just scratched the surface, is an intriguing but complicated arena. However, you should now have a basic working knowledge of the effect of changing exchange rates, the differences between appreciating and depreciating currencies, and the impact of fluctuating exchange rates on the prices of imported goods. Clearly, changing exchange rates can have a tremendous impact on the prices of imported goods, competitive prices, and international trade.

Key Terms

American terms
appreciating currency
depreciating currency
Euro
European terms
exchange rate

Name Date Section

Review Questions

Q11-1 Explain how a changing exchange rate could increase the cost of an imported product.

Q11-2 Explain the differences between American and European terms.

Q11-3 Explain what happens to the cost of foreign goods when that country's currency is:

a. appreciating.
b. depreciating.

Q11-4 List the countries that have adopted the Euro as their currency.

Name	Date	Section

Exercises

E11-1 Locate and cut out of ***your*** copy of *The Wall Street Journal* the most recent "Key Currency Cross Rates" schedule. Look in Section C. Attach it below.

Name ______ Date ______ Section ______

E11-2 a. Match the following currencies with their home country.
b. Calculate the number of foreign currency units needed to buy one US dollar.

	"Country"	Assign country letter	Currency	Units needed to buy US$1
a.	Canada	_____	pound sterling	__________
b.	Euroland	_____	C dollar	__________
c.	Japan	_____	yen	__________
d.	Mexico	_____	ringgit	__________
e.	United Kingdom	_____	Euro	__________
f.	United States	_____	peso	__________
g.	Malaysia	_____	US dollar	__________
h.	Russia	_____	ruble	__________

Name ______________________ Date ____________ Section ______

Problems/Cases

P11-1 Assume a Big Mac value meal currently costs US$3.50. How much of each of the currencies in E11-2 would be needed to buy the same meal? (Use *The Wall Street Journal* exchange rates as of ______).

"Country"	*Cost of a Big Mac*
a. Canada	____________
b. France	____________
c. Germany	____________
d. Italy	____________
e. Japan	____________
f. Mexico	____________
g. Netherlands	____________
h. Switzerland	____________
i. United Kingdom	____________
j. United States	____________
k. Malaysia	____________
l. Spain	____________
m. Russia	____________
n. Euroland	____________

Name Date Section

P11-2 In 1991, when the Lexus LS 400 was introduced, it cost $35,000 in the USA. In 1995, the equivalent model cost $50,000 in the USA. In 1997, the equivalent model cost $55,000.

a. Calculate the percentage increase in the price in US dollars:
   1. 1995 vs. 1991
   2. 1997 vs. 1995
   3. 1997 vs. 1991

b. The exchange rates in place were roughly as follows:
   1. 1991 135 yen/$
   2. 1995 80 yen/$
   3. 1997 120 yen/$

   Calculate the yen equivalent cost of a Lexus LS 400 in 1991, 1995, and 1997.

c. Calculate the percentage increase in the price in Japanese yen:
   1. 1995 vs. 1991
   2. 1997 vs. 1995
   3. 1997 vs. 1991

d. Comment on the price changes of the Lexus LS 400 since its inception in 1991, indicating which currency appreciated and which currency depreciated:
   1. 1995 vs. 1991
   2. 1997 vs. 1995
   3. 1997 vs. 1991

Materials for Further Reference

O'Brien. *Global Financial Management.* New York: John Wiley and Sons, Inc., 1996.

Harris, J. Manville, Jr. *International Finance.* Hauppauge, NY: Barron's Educational Series, Inc., 1992.

Shapiro, Alan C. *Multinational Financial Management*, 6th edition. Upper Saddle River, NJ: Prentice Hall, 1999.

Internet Web Sites to Explore

www.investorlinks.com

Chapter 12

Derivatives

Chapter Concepts

After mastering the material in this chapter, the reader will be able to:

- understand the basic nature and purposes of derivatives
- differentiate between hedgers and speculators
- identify the use of derivatives as risk minimizing tools
- identify the use of derivatives as speculative tools
- interpret options and futures data presented in *The Wall Street Journal*

Background

In investing, **derivatives** are hybrid investments. Their value, risk, etc. are "derived" from the value, risk, etc. of another investment. For example, if you think the US economy will absolutely flourish, you may want to invest in the companies who will benefit from such growth. By buying their stock, you are indirectly participating in the benefit of a growing economy. This chapter, and the accompanying chapter *in The Wall Street Journal Guide to Understanding Money and Investing*: Futures and Options, introduces the concept of derivatives and how they can be used as "risk reducers" or "risk enhancers".

Discussion

Overall, derivatives are surrogate investments, ones whose risk and value are similar to another investment. Perhaps you would like to invest in large company stocks, like those companies in the S&P 500. Unless you are extraordinarily wealthy, you probably cannot afford to buy stock in each of the 500 companies. But buying an index mutual fund that mirrors the S&P 500 will result in the same portfolio, at a much lower cost. That mutual fund is a derivative!

Derivatives have gotten a bad name, perhaps unfairly so, in the USA over the past few years. Derivatives can serve two very different purposes: to minimize risk or to leverage (or enhance) risk.

Think of nitro glycerin ... When many people think of nitro glycerin, they think of a compound used in explosives. Yet others think of how nitro glycerin may be taken orally in pill form to lower the risk associated with chest pain (angina). What a paradox! So it is with derivatives.

In a given situation, an investor in derivatives may be doing so to limit or minimize risk (like nitro glycerin in pill form for angina), investing to "hedge" a certain position. **Hedging** is a strategy to minimize risk by investing in investments that move in opposite direction. *The Wall Street Journal Guide to Understanding Money and Investing* has good examples of the use of hedging commodities with a form of derivative known as a futures contract. See p. 126 in that guide.

In another situation, an investor in derivatives may be doing so to leverage or magnify risk in hopes of a spectacular return. Whereas the "hedger" (identified in the previous example) seeks to lower risk, the "speculator" seeks to magnify risk, usually to garner huge profits. In our S&P investment example, an investor in S&P index futures would be able to indirectly purchase each of the 500 stocks (albeit a small investment in each) as a means to leverage a fewer number of dollars into a major equity holding.

Supplemental Reading

- *The Wall Street Journal Guide to Understanding Money and Investing* (1993): "Futures And Options" pp. 124 - 149

Section Outline: WSJ Guide - Futures & Options

Futures and Options

Commodities

The Futures Exchanges

Trading Futures Contracts

Hedgers and Speculators

How Futures Work

Reading Futures Tables

Financial Futures

A World of Options

Reading Options Tables

Using Options

Other Options

Tracking Other Options

Summary

Derivatives do not deserve the bad rap they often receive. If used for hedging, for example, not only are they not risky, they serve to lower other risks of the investor. A farmer may deal with derivatives to lock in a price for the crops he has just planted. As a hedger, he has eliminated the price risk fluctuations of his crops.

But speculators can use derivatives in a very risky way. Speculators are often very knowledgeable and typically proceed cautiously with such a speculative investment strategy.

Key Terms

Commodities
derivative
financial futures
futures
hedging
leverage
long positions
margin
options
short positions
speculation
spread

Name **Date** **Section**

Review Questions

Q12-1 Describe the difference between hedgers and speculators.

Q12-2 How can something inherently risky be used as a means to reduce risk?

Q12-3 Distinguish between long and short positions in futures and options.

Q12-4 Describe leverage.

Materials for Further Reference

Jarrow and Turnbull. *Derivative Securities.* Cincinnati, OH: South Western College Publishing, 1996.

Internet Web Sites to Explore

www.pitnews.com

www.investorlinks.com

www.ccsco.com\index.html

www.netcommodities.com

www.isda.org

www.numa.com

www.astrading.com

www.vt.edu:10021/business/finance/dmc/DRU/contents.html

Appendix A

Financial Institution Research

A primary goal of most individuals is financial independence. This is typically achieved through a process of *education, goal setting, planning, saving,* and *investing.*

Perhaps your *education* is starting with this studyguide/workbook! *Goal setting* requires that you establish financial objectives, end results you are shooting for. Perhaps your goal is to buy a house or retire comfortably. The *planning* aspect directs you to think about the steps necessary to reach your destination, as defined by your goals.

Any process of accumulating wealth must start with *savings.* Only with a good base of savings can investing be successful. Savings means not spending all your take-home pay, but putting some aside, in an account where risk is minimal and access is easy. Typical accounts would be bank accounts, credit union accounts, checking accounts, money market accounts, etc. While the projects in Appendices C and D deal with a simulated investing activity, we need to focus on less risky ventures first.

Financial institutions no longer have preset limits on the interest rates they pay. This is good news and bad news. The good news is that there are lots of choices available for someone starting out to establish a savings plan. The bad news is that there are SO MANY choices that a diligent effort must be put forth to make knowledgeable decisions.

What financial information would I like to have before I put money into a savings plan? Consider the following:

- risk
- rate of return
- compounding frequency
- ease of access to the funds
- convenience of location

Name	**Date**	**Section**

Assignment:

1. Select two financial institutions and compare and contrast the savings vehicles offered.

2. Complete the survey form below.

Survey form:

Institution name	____________	____________
Institution location	____________	____________
Convenience of location	____________	____________
Account type #1	____________	____________
risk	____________	____________
rate of return	____________	____________
"annual percentage yield"	____________	____________
compounding frequency	____________	____________
ease of access	____________	____________

comments:

Account type #2	______	______
risk	______	______
rate of return	______	______
"annual percentage yield"	______	______
compounding frequency	______	______
ease of access	______	______
comments:		

Account type #3	______	______
risk	______	______
rate of return	______	______
"annual percentage yield"	______	______
compounding frequency	______	______
ease of access	______	______
comments:		

Appendix B

Interpreting Investment Quotations

Background

In order to effectively understand investments, you must be able to determine their value. Values of investments are most objectively determined by finding their "quotation" or market price.

Review the following from *The Wall Street Journal Guide to Understanding Money and Investing:*

Quotes for:	Stocks	See pages:	52 - 55
	Bonds		90 - 95
	Mutual funds		114 - 117

Stock Quotes

Attach a stock page legend from *The Wall Street Journal* here.

Stocks are quoted in 1/8s and 1/16s of a dollar. While that is expected to change in the next several years to a decimal-based system, until then we need to understand and use the 100-year-old convention. The conversion to cents is listed below.

Fraction		***Decimal equivalent***
1/16	=	.0625
1/ 8	=	.125
3/16	=	.1875
1/ 4	=	.25
5/16	=	.3125
3/ 8	=	.375
7/16	=	.4375
1/ 2	=	.5
9/16	=	.5625
5/ 8	=	.625
11/16	=	.6875
3/ 4	=	.75
13/16	=	.8125
7/ 8	=	.875
15/16	=	.9375

A quote for McDonald's Corporation stock might look like this:

52 week Hi	52 week Lo	Stock	Sym	Div	Yld %	PE	Vol 100s	Hi	Lo	Close	Net Chg
52 ¼	**41**	**McDonald's**	**MCD**	**.30**	**.7**	**20**	**17975**	**44 5/8**	**44 1/8**	**44 3/8**	**+1/8**

52 Week: Hi - **$52 ¼**: indicates the highest price of this stock for the preceding 52 week period (i.e. the past year)

Lo - **$41**: indicates the lowest price of this stock for the preceding 52 week period (i.e. the past year)

Stock - **McDonald's**: company name

Sym - **MCD**: stock ticker symbol; abbreviation used to represent the company

Div - **$.30**: amount of the annual dividend (per share) paid by the company based upon the most recent declaration

Yld % - **.7%**: dividend yield: annual dividend divided by closing price, expressed as a percentage

PE - **20**: price earnings ratio: closing price divided by earnings per share reported over the last four quarters; measures the amount of money investors are willing to pay for each $1 of earnings

Vol 100s - **17975**: number of shares in 100s traded during that day's session; i.e. number of round lots (100 shares per lot) traded

Hi - **$44 5/8**: highest trading price during that day's session

Lo - **$44 1/8**: lowest trading price during that day's session

Close - **$44 3/8**: final trade price for that day's session

Net Chg - **+1/8**: change (+/-: up/down) in closing price from the previous day's closing price

Bond Quotes

A bond quote for an AT&T bond issue might look like this:

Bonds	Cur Yld	Vol	Close	Net Chg
ATT 8 1/8 24	**7.9**	**75**	**103**	**+1/8**

Bonds - **ATT**: name of issue of bond
8 1/8: annual interest rate
24: year of maturity ("2024")

Cur Yld - **7.9**%:current yield on the bond:
annual interest payment ($1,000 x 8.125% = $81.25)
divided by closing price (103 = 103% of $1,000 = $1,030)
($81.25 / $1,030 = 7.9%)

Vol - **75**: number of bonds traded during that day's session

Close - **103**: closing price of the bond, quoted in terms of percentage of $1,000 (the typical face value of a bond): 103% of $1,000 or $1,030

Net Chg -**+1/8**: net change in the closing price from the previous day's closing price; +1/8 = .00125 X 1000 = 1.25

Each day, *The Wall Street Journal* has a legend describing what various items in the bond quotes mean. Cut out a legend from the paper and attach it on this page.

Mutual Fund Quotes

A mutual fund quote for Vanguard Index 500 might look like this:

Name	NAV	Net Chg	YTD % ret
Vanguard Group			
Idx 500	**75.37**	**-0.65**	**+9.0**

Name - **Vanguard Group**: mutual fund family name, and **Idx 500**: individual fund name (abbreviated)

NAV - **$75.37**: net asset value; equivalent to closing price for a stock

Net Chg - **-0.65**: change in NAV from the previous day's session

YTD % ret -**+9.0%**: year-to-date percentage return; based upon change in NAV

Each day of the week, *The Wall Street Journal* provides slightly different information on mutual funds. The legend that appears each day in the mutual fund section explains what the quotation means. Cut out a legend from each of the five days for one week and staple them below.

Appendix C

Investment Tracking Project

Project 1: Stocks

For your high school graduation, you have just received a check for $10,000 (a gift from your grandparents) and have decided to invest the money in the stock market. Along with some friends (each of whom also received $10,000 for graduation), you have decided to pick one industry from *Value Line*. Each of you must select a different company within that industry to invest in. You and your friends have set up a contest to see whose company within the chosen industry will do best.

Project 2: Bonds

You have also received a gift certificate from your Great Aunt Helen, which entitles you to buy one bond. Choose either a corporate or government bond.

Assignments:

1. You need to write a letter to the company whose stock you have chosen to follow and obtain the following information:

   Annual Report
   Form 10-K
   any other pertinent information

   A sample letter can be found in this appendix.

2. Fill in the following information to start tracking your stock and bond.

Stock:

Industry:	____________________
Company:	____________________
Investment purchase date:	____________________
Projected investment sell date:	____________________
Shares of stock purchased:	____________________
Commission: (rate: 2% per transaction)	____________________
Market benchmark:	____________________

Bond:

Industry:	____________________
Company:	____________________
Investment purchase date:	____________________
Projected investment sell date:	____________________
Commission: (rate: 2% per transaction)	____________________

3. Track the closing prices of your stock and bond on each Tuesday and Friday (i.e. the Wednesday and Monday issues of *The Wall Street Journal*, respectively). A sample format is included at the end of this appendix. Also monitor *The Wall Street Journal* for any articles on your company(s) (focus on *The Wall Street Journal* page B-2!!) or your industry.

4. At the end of the term, your industry team must put together a creative, typed, professional presentation for the class explaining your industry, your company, and the stock performance of each company relative to an appropriate industry benchmark.

Sample letter to send requesting company information:

September 1, 1999

Mr. Joseph J. Jones
Chief Financial Officer
International Conglomerated, Incorporated
12345 Main Street
Keego Harbor, Michigan 48323

Dear Mr. Jones:

As part of my Finance course at Northwood University, my team will be tracking companies in the widget industry. I have chosen your company to follow. I will be monitoring *The Wall Street Journal* for your company's stock price and any articles relating to your company or your industry.

I would appreciate your willingness to send me the most recent issues of the following information on your company:

> Annual Report
> Form 10-K
> Form 10-Q
> Proxy Statement

Any other information you think would be valuable to me would be most welcomed.

Northwood University is a private, accredited college specializing in managerial and entrepreneurial education. The college emphasizes the importance of free enterprise and is dedicated to the preservation of the free market and the important relationship between business and the arts.

If you would like a copy of my team's final project, please let me know.

Sincerely,

Mary E. Smith
Northwood University
Class of 2001

cc: Mr. Mark J. Minbiole
Chairman: Banking and Finance Department
Northwood University

______________________________ _____________ ______

Name **Date** **Section**

I have chosen the following stock and bond for the Investment Tracking Projects:

Stock Tracking Project:	***Bond*** Tracking Project
Industry:________________	Industry:__________________
Company:______________	Company:________________
Stock purchase date:______	Bond purchase date:_______
Stock price:______________	Bond price:________________
Shares purchased:________	Bonds purchased:__________
Commission paid:_________	Commission paid:__________
Total cost: $10,000	Total cost:________________

Sample Format: Investment Tracking Form

Date	Stock shares X	Stock price =	Stock value +	Bond value =	Total value

Appendix D

Company Information Disclosure Project

<u>Project:</u> Congratulations! You have just been promoted to Financial Reporting Analyst of your company. Your new responsibilities include filing a "Disclosure Statement" (FORM F-100) with the Commissioner (your professor) of the ITA ("Investment Trading Agency"). Use the table of contents below to develop your company's disclosure statement. Note: disclosure is the process of presenting reliable, timely, relevant, and consistent information to investors so they can make informed decisions as to whether to buy, sell or hold stock in the company.

International Conglomerate, Inc.
FORM F-100
Table of Contents

Cover

Table of Contents

Executive Summary

Business Background

Stock Performance

Selected Financial Data

In the News

Exhibits / Appendices

Sources:

To complete the disclosure statement, locate and obtain information from such financial information sources as: company annual reports, Form 10-K, The Wall Street Journal, your professor, the Internet, previous FORM F-100 filings, etc.

Tools:

Use word processing, spreadsheet, and graphics to complete your project.

Format:

See example blank FORM F-100 on the following pages. Because the ITA is very strict on what is included in the disclosure statement, it has developed FORM F-100 as a non-negotiable format to present your company's information. Use creativity within the boundaries of FORM F-100's requirements.

FORMF100A

FORM F-100

INVESTMENT AND TRADING AGENCY
MIDLAND, MICHIGAN 48640

FOR THE TERM: ______________ **FINANCIAL DATA AS OF:** ______________
TRACKING DATA AS OF: ______________

INTERNATIONAL CONGLOMERATED, INC

(exact name of registrant)
12345 Main Street
Keego Harbor, Michigan 48323
(248) 555-9876

TYPE OF ORGANIZATION **"C" CORPORATION**

TYPE OF STOCK **EXCHANGE WHERE CURRENTLY TRADED**

COMMON STOCK **NEW YORK STOCK EXCHANGE**

CURRENT VALUE: _______ **STOCK SYMBOL:** _________

PAR VALUE: _______ **BENCHMARK:** **STANDARD & POORS 500**

SHARES OUTSTANDING: ______

PREPARED BY:
YOUR NAME
FINANCIAL ANALYST
3225 Cook Rd.
Miner 00
Midland, MI 48640
(517) 837-4400

SUBMITTED TO:
PROFESSOR'S NAME
COMMISSIONER
3225 Cook Rd.
GSAB 108
Midland, MI 489640
(517) 837-4200

INTERNATIONAL CONGLOMERATED, INC.
TABLE OF CONTENTS

INTERNATIONAL CONGLOMERATED, INC.
EXECUTIVE SUMMARY

COMPANY PROFILE

COMPETITION

STOCK PERFORMANCE VS. BENCHMARK

- $$$
- %%%

FINANCIAL SUMMARY

- Sales
- Assets
- Net Income
- Cash from Operations
- Other

ECONOMIC STATISTICS

- GDP Growth
- CPI
- Unemployment
- 30 Year Treasury Bond Rate
- 90 Day Treasury Bill Rate

INTERNATIONAL CONGLOMERATED, INC.
BUSINESS BACKGROUND

HISTORY

INDUSTRY

PRODUCTS/SERVICES

COMPETITION

SOURCES OF RISK

SUBSIDIARIES

LOCATIONS

EXECUTIVE OFFICERS
- **CHAIRMAN**
- **CEO**
- **PRESIDENT**
- **COO**
- **CFO**

INTERNATIONAL CONGLOMERATED, INC.
STOCK PERFORMANCE

Performance Summary:

Performance Tracking:

CLOSING DATE	*STOCK PRICE*	*SHARES TRADED*	*RIVAL PRICE*	*BENCHMARK LEVEL #1*	*BENCHMARK LEVEL #2*

Gains / Losses:

Graphs:

INTERNATIONAL CONGLOMERATED, INC.
SELECTED FINANCIAL DATA

CONDENSED BALANCE SHEETS

	1998	1997		1998	1997
Current Assets			Current Liabilities		
Fixed Assets, net			Other Liabilities		
Other Assets	____	____	Stockholders' Equity	____	____
Total			Total		

CONDENSED INCOME STATEMENTS

	1998	1997	1996
Net Sales/Revenues			
Cost of Sales	____	____	____
Gross Profit			
Other Expenses	____	____	____
Net Income			
Earnings per Share			
Dividends per Share			

CONDENSED CASH FLOW STATEMENTS

	1998	1997	1996
Cash from Operating Activities			
Cash from Investing Activities			
Cash from Financing Activities	____	____	____
Net Cash Flow			
Cash: Beginning of Year	____	____	____
Cash: End of Year			

INTERNATIONAL CONGLOMERATED, INC.
IN THE NEWS

ARTICLE #1

ARTICLE #2

ARTICLE #3

INTERNATIONAL CONGLOMERATED, INC.
EXHIBITS / APPENDICES

Appendix E

Teams: Concepts and Evaluations

It seems as though throughout your school years, you have been told to "do your own work". Yet in business, individual performance AND team performance are each important.

By way of illustration, consider a 400 meter track and field relay team. Both individual performance and team performance are crucial ingredients for victory. Yet, while a runner is running s/he must do it alone, except perhaps for some encouragement from teammates.

But sometimes on a team, there are members who don't carry their own weight: "laggards".

Your term-long project will be graded as a team with one modification: for any individual team member, his/her score will be the team score multiplied by a "team evaluation factor", an average of the scores provided by each team member for each member of the team.

The "team evaluation factor" is computed as follows:

1. Multiply the number of team members by 100.
2. Allocate this total number of points to the team members (including yourself) on the basis of contribution to the team's performance.
3. No team member can be given more than 150 points.
4. Remember, if you allocate more than 100 points to someone, someone else must get fewer than 100 points!!
5. The team evaluation factors determined for each team member are summed up and averaged.

This team evaluation factor, when converted to a percentage, is multiplied by the team project score to arrive at an individual's point total for the project.

Example: A team consisting of Craig, Paul, Barry, and Brian select the Banking industry. They do their project and receive, let's say, 95 out of 100 points from the Professor. The team evaluation form results were as follows:

Rating by ◊ Rating for: II V	***Craig***	***Paul***	***Barry***	***Brian***	***Avg.***
Craig	100	100	100	100	100
Paul	105	105	95	95	100
Barry	120	90	100	130	110
Brian	75	105	105	75	90
Total	400	400	400	400	400

Note: The professor will compute all averages and keep the team evaluation form information strictly confidential. In this example, Craig and Paul will each get 100% of the 95 total team project points: 95. Barry will get 110% of the 95 total team project points: 104.5. Brian will get 90% of the 95 total team project points: 85.5.

TEAM EVALUATION FORM

Course:______________________________________ Section:____

Team name:__________________________________ Date:_______

Team members	Score	Comments
___________________	____	____________________________
___________________	____	____________________________
___________________	____	____________________________
___________________	____	____________________________
___________________	____	____________________________
___________________	____	____________________________
___________________	____	____________________________
___________________	____	____________________________
___________________	____	____________________________
___________________	____	____________________________
___________________	____	____________________________
___________________	____	____________________________
Total Points	____	(total points must equal number of team members times 100)

Appendix F

Financial Mathematics*

Annualized Return =(yield / months held) x 12

Basic earnings per share = net earnings / outstanding shares of common stock

Book value per share = $\frac{\text{(common stock + capital surplus + retained earnings)}}{\text{number of outstanding shares}}$

Break-even sales dollars = variable costs + fixed costs

Capital appreciation = (current price - purchase price) / purchase price

Compounding

Daily = annual rate / 365

Monthly = annual rate / 12

Coupon rate = annual interest payment / maturity value of the bond

Current bond yield = annual interest payment / current bond price

Diluted earnings per share = $\frac{\text{(net earnings + conversion value)}}{\text{outstanding shares after conversion}}$

Discount yield = (discount amount / face value) x (360 / days to maturity)

Dividend yield = annual dividend / current stock price

Earnings rate after tax = gross earnings rate (100 - tax rate)

Future value of $1 = $(1 + \text{interest rate})^{\text{number of periods}}$
= PV x FVIF = present value x future value interest factor

Future value of an annuity of $1

FV = annuity$[((1 + \text{interest rate})^{\text{number of periods}} - 1) / \text{interest rate}]$
= A x FVIFA = annuity x future value interest factor for annuity

Interest = principal x interest rate x time

Net asset value = (market value + cash on hand) / number of shares outstanding

Net earnings = net income minus preferred dividends

Payout ratio = dividends on common stock / net earnings

Present value of $1 = 1 / (1 + interest rate)$^{\text{number of periods}}$
= FV x PVIF = future value x present value interest factor

Present value of an annuity of $1

PV = annuity[(1 -1/(1 + interest rate)$^{\text{number of periods}}$) / interest rate]
= A x PVIFA = annuity x present value interest factor for an annuity

Present value of bond =

face value / (1 + interest rate for half-year)$^{\text{number of half-year periods}}$

Price earnings ratio = market price / earnings per share

Return on invested capital =

<u>(net income + interest expense)</u>
(shareholders' equity + par value of long-term bonds)

Rule of 72 (number of years required to double principal) = 72 / interest rate

Yield = annual interest payment / current market price

Yield to maturity =
(Interest + ((Principal - Price) / Years)) / ((Price x 60%) + (Principal x 40%))

*Sources: Thomsett, Michael C. *The Mathematics of Investing.* New York: John Wiley & Sons, Inc., 1989

Other

Appendix G

The Wall Street Journal Publication Schedule for Key Government Statistics

(Source: *The Wall Street Journal Workbook*, Michael B. Lehmann, 5th Edition)

Day of Month/Week Usually Published in *The Wall Street Journal*	Series Description	Quarterly Monthly Weekly Daily
Middle of last month of quarter	Balance of payments	quarterly
25th	GDP	quarterly
month after end of quarter	Productivity	quarterly
1st	Leading indicators	monthly
1st week	Consumer confidence	monthly
1st week	Manufacturer's orders	monthly
5th, 15th, 25th	New vehicle sales	monthly
Monday of 2nd week	Employment	monthly
2nd week	Consumer credit	monthly
Middle of 2nd week	Retail sales	monthly
Midmonth	Industrial production	monthly
Midmonth	Capacity utilization	monthly
Midmonth	Producer price index	monthly
Midmonth	Consumer price index	monthly
17th to 20th	Housing starts	monthly
3rd week	Balance of trade	monthly
Thursday or Friday of next-to last week	Durable goods orders (nondefense capital goods)	monthly
4th week	Inventories	monthly
Last week	Federal expenditures, receipts, deficit	monthly
Last week	Personal income	monthly
Monday	Bond yields (chart)	weekly
Tuesday	Treasury Bill auction	weekly
Thursday	Short-term interest rates (chart)	weekly
Friday	Federal Reserve data	weekly
Monday-Friday	Foreign exchange rates	daily
Monday-Friday	Treasury bill rates	daily

Appendix H

Glossary

AMEX (American Stock Exchange) - US stock exchange for mid-sized companies, especially financial and natural resources firms.

American terms - an exchange rate quoted as US dollars per foreign currency, such as the pound sterling.

annual report - document written by company management designed to summarize the prior year's financial and business activities. It usually includes letter to shareholders, company information, and financial statements.

appreciating currency - currency strengthening with changes in the exchange rate.

Balance Sheet - a snapshot of a company's financial position as of a point in time. It shows what the company owns and owes, and its net worth.

barter - goods given in exchange for other goods.

Beige book – a region-by-region look at the US economy named for the color of its cover, produced by the Federal Reserve

benchmarking - process of measuring results against a standard.

blue chips - stocks of the largest, most consistently profitable corporations.

bond - any interest-bearing or discounted government or corporate security that obligates the issuer to pay the bondholder a specified sum of money, usually at specific intervals, and to repay the principal amount of the loan at maturity.

bond funds - mutual funds that invest in bonds. These funds may be tax-free or taxable. They have no maturity date and no guaranteed repayment of invested amounts.

boom - general direction of the economy is up.

business cycle - recurrence of periods of expansion (recovery) and contraction (recession) in economic activity with effects on inflation, growth, and employment. One cycle extends from a GNP base line through one rise and one decline and back to the base line, a period averaging about 2 ½ years. A business cycle affects profitability and cash flow, making it a key consideration in corporate dividend policy, and is a factor in the rise and fall of the inflation rate, which in turn affects return on investment.

bust - general direction of the economy is down.

buying on margin - investor sets up an account with broker and borrows up to 50% of total price of stock to make a purchase.

CPI - see consumer price index.

C Corporation - typical corporate form of business with unlimited shareholders, limited liability, and corporate responsibility for income taxes.

capital gains - profit made from selling stock at a higher price than when it was purchased.

Cash Flow Statement - financial statement that reflects an historical view of company's sources and uses of cash for a period of time.

Chairman of the Federal Reserve - head central banker of the USA. Nominated by the President and confirmed by Congress.

closed funds - mutual funds not open to new investors.

closed end funds - mutual funds that raise money only once, offer fixed number of shares, and are traded on an exchange.

commodities - raw materials, such as wheat, silver, oil, sugar, and money.

common stock - ownership shares in a corporation.

consumer price index (CPI) - index that reflects the change in consumer prices from one year to the next on a market basket of goods.

Consumption - personal expenditures portion of GDP measured by purchases of food, clothing, shelter, services, vehicles, and other durable goods.

corporate bonds - bonds sold by corporations, usually to raise cash for expansion, operations, acquisitions, or restructuring. They are traded on the NYSE or AMEX and are rated based on risk associated with corporation's financial stability.

corporation - form of business with limited liability, transferability of ownership, and taxation.

coupon rate - interest rate on a bond.

cumulative voting - shareholders receive one vote for each board of director opening for each share owned. These votes may be split anyway shareholder chooses. This form of voting is required by some states.

currency - money used to obtain goods and services.

cyclical stocks - share of companies whose stock prices changes with the economy, up or down.

data - financial, economic, and statistical amounts that must be analyzed and interpreted for use in decision making.

debentures - unsecured corporate bonds, backed by credit of issuing corporation.

depreciating currency - currency weakening with changes in the exchange rate.

derivative - a hybrid investment whose value is derived from the value of another investment.

discount bonds - bonds issued at interest rate below the market rate. Proceeds from the sale of such a bond would be less than the face value of the bond.

dividend yield - percentage of purchase price of stock returned in dividends each year.

dividends - portion of corporation's profit paid out to its shareholders.

divisibility of ownership - in a corporation, ownership units are based on a single unit that can be accumulated in different quantities.

double taxation - corporation's income is taxed twice when it pays dividends. The corporation pays income taxes on profits before dividends and the shareholders pay income taxes on the amount of dividends received.

Dow Jones Industrial Average (DJIA) - US stock market average calculated using thirty stocks and a simple average.

Exports - the part of GDP that represents the money received for USA products and services shipped outside its boundaries.

economic cycle - the increases in demand and prices (inflation) that lead to decreases in demand and prices (recession) that then cause the cycle of increases and decreases to begin again.

Euro - a currency unit used effective 1/1/99 by 11 member countries in Europe for non-physical currency transactions, replacing these countries' respective sovereign currencies for said purposes

European terms - an exchange rate quoted as foreign currency per US dollar.

exchange rate - rate at which one can buy one currency with another currency.

federal deficit - excess of federal government spending over federal government tax revenues.

federal reserve - national system of twelve banks, governed by 17 member Board of Governors, established by Congress to keep financial systems stable.

financial futures - currencies, stock and bonds indexes, and interest rate contracts traded on exchanges.

fixed income security - also known as a bond - pays fixed amount of interest regularly and principal amount at maturity.

free enterprise system - an environment that places responsibility for managing one's affairs on the individual with little or no governmental intervention.

futures - obligations to buy or sell a specific commodity on a specific day for a specific price.

GAAP - see generally accepted accounting principles.

GDP - see gross domestic product.

GTC (Good 'til canceled) - order with broker that stands until filled or canceled by investor.

generally accepted accounting principles (GAAP) - rules, procedures, and guidelines followed in preparing financial statements and related information.

geometric average - calculating an index using a complicated mathematical model that adjusts index for each change in individual stock price.

global funds - mutual funds that includes stocks and bonds from the USA and other countries.

Government spending - measure of federal, state, and local governmental expenditures, exclusive of transfer payments, that is included in GDP.

Gross Domestic Product (GDP) - measures changes in economic activity of final output of all goods and services produced in United States. It is quoted quarterly as annual percentage change from previous quarter in spending components of Consumption, Investment, Government, and Net Exports.

growth stocks - stocks that pay little or no dividend while reinvesting profits, hoping for substantial price appreciation.

hedging - strategy to minimize risk by investing in financial instruments that move in opposite directions.

IPO (initial public offering)- first time stock or bonds of a company are offered for sale to the public.

Imports - part of GDP that includes money paid by US consumers for goods and services provided from outside the United States.

Income Statement - financial statement that provides historical view of the company's revenues and expenses for a period of time.

index - standard against which financial performance is compared.

inflation - percent price change for similar goods/services from year to year.

information - data that has value to the user.

intermediate-term bonds - bonds sold with a maturity of two to ten years.

international funds - mutual funds that invest in foreign stock and bond markets.

Internet - electronic source of information, accessed via computer

inventory change - net increase or decrease in businesses' stocks during quarter which is used in the calculation of GDP.

Investment - measure of long-term business and consumer purchases and net change in business inventory for the quarter which is part of GDP.

investment clubs - groups of investors who pool their funds and make consensus investment decisions.

investment objectives - basic goals for mutual fund investment that fit in one of three basic categories: current income, future growth, or both growth and income.

junk bonds - lowest rated corporate bonds that carry high risk issuer will fail to pay its debt.

LEI - see leading economic indicators.

LLC (limited liability company) - functions like S Corporation without limit to number of shareholders.

LLP (limited liability partnership) - partnership that minimizes unlimited liability for most partners.

leading economic indicators (LEI) - set of 11 key statistics that tend to move up or down ahead of GDP, thus making them predictors of what is to come in the business cycle.

leverage - investing with money borrowed at a fixed rate of interest in hope of earning greater rate of return.

limit order - specific amount investor identifies to a broker for when to buy (only when it falls to this price) and sell (only when it climbs to this pre-established price).

limited liability - maximum liability is amount invested.

long positions - ownership position established by an investor.

long-term bonds - bonds sold with a maturity of ten years or more.

MD&A (management's discussion and analysis) - management's explanation of why financial numbers are different from one year to the next.

M1 (narrow money) - includes all cash and money in checking accounts.

M2 (broad money) - includes M1 plus savings accounts, time deposits, and money market funds/accounts.

M3 - includes M1 and M2 plus assets and liabilities, including long-term deposits, of financial institutions.

management - *noun:* leadership team of an enterprise.

management - *verb*: the process of finding and fixing problems through others to maximize the value of the company for the benefit of its shareholders.

margin - buying stock using some of one's own money and up to 50% borrowed from a broker.

market capitalization - stock price per share times number of shares outstanding.

market order - instruction to a broker that says buy or sell at the best price at the moment.

maturity date - date loan/bond expires and must be paid back in full.

mid caps - stocks with market capitalization in the $1 - 5 billion range.

money - value exchanged for goods and/or services received.

money cycle - the process of replacing existing bills and coins that wear out.

money market accounts/funds - taxable or tax-free mutual funds in which one dollar is returned with interest for every dollar invested.

money supply - measurement of amount of money that people have available to spend.

municipal bonds - bonds issued by cities, towns and counties that are exempted from federal income taxes.

mutual fund - an investment company for the purpose of offering its shareholders a specific investment objective.

mutual fund family - mutual funds with different investment objectives owned by the same advisory firm.

NASDAQ - network run by National Association of Securities Dealers as a stock market, particularly for smaller, emerging companies.

NYSE (New York Stock Exchange) - US stock market exchange for largest companies.

Nominal GDP (current dollar GDP) - measure of actual change in dollar spending, including impact of changing prices.

non-residential investment - business purchases of long-lived assets included in GDP.

odd lot - buying and selling shares of stock in amounts more or less than even 100 share increments.

open funds - mutual funds that accept new investors.

open end funds - mutual funds with no limit as to the number of shares to be sold.

options - right to buy or sell a specific item for a preset price during a specific period of time.

ownership transfer - selling all or part of ownership position in stock or bond.

par value - dollar amount of a bond or preferred stock at time it will mature.

partnership - business owned by two or more individuals in which partners take full responsibility for legal obligations of company, including income taxes.

personal responsibility - concept that individuals are accountable for their own actions and well being.

preferred stock - ownership shares of a company with reduced risk and limited reward compared to common stock.

premium - bond issued at interest rate above the market rate. Proceeds from the sale of such a bond would be more than the face value of the bond.

prorata form - division of losses and profits of partnership among partners based on agreement.

prospectus - legal document available to anyone investing in initial offerings of stocks and bonds.

Proxy - absentee ballot for shareholders unable to attend a corporation's annual meeting.

Proxy Statement - document issued to all shareholders that includes issues to be voted on at a corporation's annual meeting, information on the Board of Directors, officers, compensation, and stock performance.

ratings - classifications of risk assumed by the purchaser of bonds based on a third-party evaluation of the financial condition of the bond issuer.

Real GDP (constant dollar GDP) - measure of actual change in output, exclusive of the impact of inflation.

recession - slow down in the economy commenced by two consecutive quarters of negative GDP growth.

residential investment - amount spent by consumers on purchase of newly-built homes which is included in GDP.

right to vote - right given to shareholders to voice their opinion on major policy decision.

round lot - buying and selling stock in multiples of 100 shares.

S Corporation - corporation with no more than 75 shareholders and limited liability that has made the election to have its shareholders taxed as if it were a partnership.

SEC - see Securities and Exchange Commission

SEC Forms:

8-K - informational report required to be filed when major corporate news takes place.

10-K - annual report filed within 90 days of year-end that includes information about the company, legal proceedings, and financial statements.

10-Q - quarterly report filed within 45 days of the end of the quarter updating financial information about company.

Securities and Exchange Commission (SEC) - government agency whose mission is to ensure adequate information is available to investors.

shareholder value - value of corporation to its owners.

shareholders - individuals and institutions owning positions of a corporation. Also called stockholders.

short positions - borrowed shares of stocks from broker that must be repaid like a loan.

short selling - borrowing shares from broker, selling them and getting cash.

short-term bonds - bonds sold with a maturity of one year or less.

simple average - calculating an index by adding value of one unit of each component in the index and dividing by a factor.

small caps - stocks with a market capitalization of less than $1 billion.

sole proprietorship - business owned by only one person.

speculation - rumor, inside information, or other factors that influence commodity's price up or down.

spread - difference between two contracts' prices.

Standard & Poors - stock index tracking organization and rating service for bond investors.

stock certificate - paper record of information about share(s) owned by a shareholder.

stock dividend - return of corporation's profits to its shareholders in the form of additional shares of stock.

stock funds - mutual funds that invest primarily in stocks that offer no guaranteed repayments of invested amounts.

stock quotations - current stock price and trading details identified by a corporation's trading symbol.

stock split - corporation issues a multiple of shares for each share currently held. It usually occurs when the price of a share gets too high to attract buyers.

stockholders - individuals and institutions owning positions of a corporation. Also called shareholders.

term structure of interest rates - relationship among short-term, intermediate-term, and long-term interest rates of government securities, depicted by a yield curve, as of a point in time.

third-party information provider - businesses in the information industry that obtain data and package it for others, usually for a fee.

trade deficit - when United States trade imports exceed its exports.

US Government Agency bonds - bonds issued by federal agencies, such as Ginnie Mae, Fannie Mae, and Freddie Mac.

US Treasury bonds - bonds issued by the federal government with maturities greater than ten years.

unemployment - percentage of unemployed Americans actively seeking employment.

Value Line - stock index tracking organization and rating service for stock investors.

value-weighted average - calculating an index by valuing each item in the index and dividing by a factor.

yield-to-maturity - value to be earned by holder of financial instrument if it is held until maturity.

yield curve - graphical depiction of relationship between short-term, intermediate-term, and long-term interest rates

zero coupon bonds - bonds sold at a discount that pay no periodic interest. The interest accumulates until maturity.

Index

F

G

H

I

J

K

L

M

N

O

P

R

S

T

U

V

W

Y

Z